The Famous Five

Emily Murphy and the Case of the Missing Persons

Nancy Millar

Published by:
The Western Heritage Centre
P.O. Box 1477
Cochrane, Alberta
T0L 0W0

Printed in Cochrane, Alberta, Canada

Graphic Design by Kris Nielson
Front Cover Photograph, "Emily Murphy"
Courtesy of The City of Edmonton Archives / EA-10-1996

NATIONAL LIBRARY OF CANADA
CATALOGUING IN PUBLICATION DATA

The Western Heritage Centre

The Famous Five
Emily Murphy and the Case of the Missing Persons
by Nancy Millar

Includes biographical references and index
ISBN 0-9685962-0-7
1. Women - Alberta - Canada - History.   2. Law - Alberta - Canada - History

The Famous Five

Emily Murphy and the Case of the Missing Persons

Nancy Millar

contents

introduction

The Famous Five

Not one word did I hear in my school days about the Famous Five women from Alberta. Granted, my school days are long gone but my daughters didn't hear about them either, and my daughters are young. Why don't we know these wonderful women? Why can't we say their names without hesitation?

Emily Murphy
Nellie McClung
Henrietta Muir Edwards
Irene Parlby
Louise McKinney

Right in my own back yard, in the province of Alberta, they pulled off one of the biggest legal coups ever. Without a referendum or a royal commission or a federal election, they changed the meaning of Section 24 of the British North America Act. By so doing, they changed the Canadian constitution, which in turn changed Canadian women into persons who could become senators. They were persons before that in the common meaning of the word, but they weren't person enough to be appointed to the Senate.

It doesn't make sense, but that's what the Persons Case was all about…how to define a "person" as the word was used in Section 24 of the BNA Act. Out on the street, the word "persons" meant both men and women, of course, but the BNA Act was a legal document. As such, it was based on British common law, and British common law had some different ideas about who was a person and who was not.

Not many women knew or cared about this confusion within our law. When I told my mother, for instance, that she wasn't a person until she was 18 years old, she said, "Don't be silly. Of course, I was a person. What was I if I wasn't a person?"

Good question, mom, but the fact remains that for awhile the BNA Act did not define her as a whole person. Just a part person. Most women were like my mother. They didn't know they weren't persons and didn't much care about the words used. What could they do anyway other than get up every morning and make the best of their lives? Or to paraphrase Emily Murphy, what could they do other than make butter, make hay, make meals, make beds and at all times in between make good? Women didn't have a lot of time for introspection; they had to get on with daily life. So legal personhood wasn't a huge issue, not for most women. It was too removed from the reality of their lives.

It was, however, a huge issue for Emily Murphy. She heard over and over again in her Edmonton courtroom that she wasn't a person. On top of that, three prime ministers and five different federal government administrations told her she wasn't a person, so she couldn't be a senator. And as if she needed any more proof that women weren't persons, she saw women day after day in her courtroom who had no sense of themselves as persons, legal or otherwise.

No wonder she snapped. Thank goodness she snapped.

Here then follows the story of the Famous Five women from Alberta and the Persons Case, complete with courtroom drama, love and hate, original intent, fallen women, temptation, perturbation, one big broken heart and five big-hearted splendid women, er, persons.

chapter one

The Famous One - Emily Murphy

The Famous Five were Emily Murphy, Nellie McClung, Irene Parlby, Louise McKinney and Henrietta Muir Edwards. All of them were from Alberta, all of them were formidable in their own right. But even as they're referred to as the Famous Five, it must be admitted that they were actually the Famous One Plus Four. This is what Emily Murphy's daughter said years later in a note to a friend still living in Edmonton:

> I must say it riles me when they talk of the "Famous Five" when all the other four women did was to allow their names to stand with mother's in her appeal to the Privy Council. She did all the rest on her own. I know because I typed the letters. The four others only lent their names to one petition but paid none of the costs, nor did any of the work in taking the case through the different courts. But now they are the "Famous Five." It's really funny.

She was right. Her mother was indeed the ringleader in the Persons Case. Canadian women might still be constitutional non-persons had Emily not got tired of the "same old rigmarole" in her courtroom one day and decided to do something about it. After all, it was she who liked to say, "Whenever I don't know whether to fight or not, I fight." Still, Emily needed both the muscle and the moral support of the other four. She couldn't have done it on her own.

Born to the well-known and well-placed Ferguson family of Cookstown, Ontario, Emily was a "person" to be reckoned with from the very beginning. No way would she let her brothers beat

"Whenever I don't know whether to fight or not, I fight." - Emily Murphy

Emily Murphy became the first woman police magistrate in the British Empire.
(c. 1916)

Photo Courtesy Glenbow Archives
NA-273-3

her at anything including the carving of the Sunday roast, a task normally reserved for the males of the family. Emily demanded equal time at the table and her sympathetic father agreed. Everyone should know how to carve a roast, he said. "The idea that she was just a girl and therefore for some reason less capable than the boys never entered her head," he said in a conversation many years later.

At age 19, she married a young Anglican priest, Arthur Murphy, and threw all her considerable energy into being the model minister's wife. In parishes across southern Ontario and for awhile in England, she joined women's groups, taught Sunday School, typed up Arthur's sermons, now and then told Arthur what to say, visited the parishioners and generally had a fine time. Even the birth of Kathleen and Evelyn didn't break her stride, but the day she fell downstairs was the beginning of a more difficult period for the Murphy family. Madeleine was born prematurely as the result of the fall and never quite got a hold on life. She died at nine months of age. Then the fourth daughter Doris, the apple of her mother's eye, died of diphtheria when she was 10 years old. It happened so quickly that Arthur didn't even have time to get there from one of his rural Ontario missions. Emily was alone with Doris when she died, and she grieved for her always.

Among her daughter's things, she found a sampler, the sort of needlework that young girls did in those days. It said simply, "Be good." Emily wrote later, "It is the summary of my creed. I know other and longer ones but they may all be reduced to these words. After all, creeds do not differ; it is only the people."

By this time, Emily had begun her writing career. Enroute by boat to England a few years earlier, she had overheard a British woman making disparaging remarks about "Canucks." They were hopeless rubes, the British woman confided to her friends, terribly similar to Americans. Rather than taking offence, Emily decided that anything that bad had to have some merit. So she took the name Canuck, added Janey, and came up with her pen name, Janey Canuck. And when her first book, *Impressions of Janey Canuck Abroad*, won high praise from certain British reviewers, she had the last word.

Her second book was called *Janey Canuck in the West* because by that time the Murphy family had moved to Swan River, Manitoba. Arthur left the ministry to start a business in timber and real estate. Four years later they were on the move again.

"The Padre has decided to live in Edmonton and I have decided to remain in Swan River. We will compromise on Edmonton," Emily explained ruefully, but as it turned out, Edmonton, Alberta, suited her wonderfully. In 1907, it wasn't yet a place that worried a great deal about Who's Who and Who's Not, so it was a great place to mix with all kinds of people and learn all sorts of things. For instance, while her husband talked land business with farmers around Edmonton, she got to talk to the wives, and what she learned opened a whole new world to her. From a privileged background where women were protected by custom, if not law, she learned about women not protected by law or custom.

One woman told her how she'd been washing clothes one afternoon when a wagonload of people and goods drove into the yard. "Why are you still here?" the driver asked. It turned out that her husband had sold the property but had neglected to tell her, a neglect that was perfectly legal at that time. There were no property laws on the books that protected a wife's interest in the family home or even gave her the right to know of transactions involving her home.

Emily couldn't believe her ears. That's when she became a regular at the library in the legislative buildings. "Can this be true?" she'd ask the librarians and then read until she found out. Eventually, she met and worked with Henrietta Muir Edwards of Fort Macleod, Alberta, who seemed to know most everything there was to know about laws as they related to women and children. As the convener of laws for the National Council of Women, she too saw the need for a Dower Act, an act that would protect women in the disposition of family property.

Letters like this one added to their determination to do something. Written in a strong hand, there's every sign throughout this long letter that the writer was an educated women, but she dared not name herself. Instead she signed: Western Canadian Wife.

Dear Madam,
    Seeing the notice in the Free Press re Dower Act for Alberta, I think it is time we did have such a law. I don't understand quite what the Dower Act is, but I'm thinking that it is a law giving married women a lawful right to half of everything that her husband owns – lands, houses and moveable property of all kinds. Is that so? My husband has all along let me understand that one-third of his estate goes to the wife, two-thirds to his children at his death. But now I am convinced that I might get nothing and that he might give his all away from me and my young family of seven. I must say that he has threatened to do so whenever any little thing crosses him. Now, I left all my friends and comforts and society and came to this new country and had many lonely, trying times, endured many hardships including hunger and cold.

Have had to do all kinds of work outdoors in all kinds of weather – chop wood, carry water, milk cows, feed horses and cattle, feed pigs, etc., all sorts of work that a hired man would have to do, besides all the baking, cooking, washing and housework for a large family and without the modern contrivances of labor saving machinery. Also, most of my children's clothes I make besides most of my own and my husband's. My husband owns half a section of good land and hires no help. I help in the haying and harvest, plant along with my children (the oldest is only ten years old) more than an acre of potatoes which we all gather in the fall. I do all that and lots more which I know most women around me would not dream of doing. I am seldom from home, never get to church or a party. No pleasure or company of any kind. The reason I could not invite anyone to come and spend an afternoon, I am always kept so full of work, and my house though large has no furniture of any kind but a stove, table and chairs –only two. I have not even a rocker to sit down my weary body and tired back. I have nothing but the bare necessities of life.

If I thought that I had to live my life out like this, I think I would go crazy but I have great hopes and that, with my trust in God, keeps me going. But it would be a great comfort and security for most women to be assured that if her husband died, something would be hers to start with, especially a woman who helps her husband…

Shame on the farmers of Western Canada – they cry for Equity Associations, Good and Honest. But how few of them would ever think of being Even and Equal with the wife of his Bosom.

Western Canadian Wife

"Matrimony is the only game of chance the clergy favour."
- Emily Murphy

Shame on everybody, for that matter. No wonder Emily got busier than ever with her research and her lobbying. The word "lobbying" had not yet been invented in the early 1900s but Emily could do it, whatever it was called. Because she was one of the "right" sort, she could speak to others of the "right" sort – government and community leaders, the society of Edmonton. It didn't always work, of course. Enroute to the Dower Act, she appealed to the Attorney General of Alberta, Charles W. Cross. His response to her request for a bill that would protect women was, "Why should women worry about possessing some of their husband's property during his lifetime? Time enough after he's dead."

R.B. Bennett, then a young MLA from Calgary and later the Prime Minister of Canada, finally agreed to introduce a bill in the legislature for which trouble he was labelled as "a susceptible young man affected by the pleadings of the ladies." And in spite of that selfsame pleading – Emily Murphy delivered a 90-minute speech on behalf of it – the bill was thrown out.

That was in 1910. Emily Murphy had not been in Edmonton that long. She had not been involved in social causes that often, but she was so sure that this was the right thing at the right time that a newspaper reporter said, "Mrs. Murphy is so much in earnest over the bill that its success is as good as accomplished."

He was right. The Married Women's Protective Act (1911) was passed by the Alberta legislature the next year. It wasn't nearly as comprehensive as Emily and others would have liked it to be, but it was a start in that it assured wives of one-third of a husband's estate upon his death, no matter what the will said.

One disgruntled politician was heard to remark, "Don't let Mrs. Murphy in; all she does is make trouble."

He was right. Emily seemed to turn up everywhere. She continued to work on dower rights. She urged that women be part of local school boards. She pressed for women to be appointed to hospital boards and then put her money where her mouth was and became the first woman on an Edmonton hospital board. She convinced the Victorian Order of Nurses to extend their services to Edmonton. She prodded city fathers about playground space and public hygiene standards. She joined the fight for women's suffrage – that was fun – and then she became a police magistrate – that wasn't so much fun.

What happened was this. Several members of the Local Council of Women (LCW), an eminently respectable group of women concerned with legal and social conditions for women and children, attended court one day. While they were there, a case involving prostitution came up, and because the details would be too rough for the ears of "decent women," the judge asked the LCW members to leave.

Confused and annoyed, they told their story to Emily Murphy who promptly paid a visit to the Attorney General. Why in the world ask the women to leave when the case involved women, she demanded? Surely it would make more sense to ask the men to leave. Surely it would make more sense to have an all-woman's court, for that matter, she concluded, with a female judge to hear cases involving females.

Good idea, the Attorney General replied, and within days asked her to take on the job as police magistrate for a newly organized women's court. The Attorney General was no dummy. He knew a good thing when he saw it. He also knew he had Emily over a barrel. She had asked for a special court; she couldn't easily say no. Besides, she'd be the first woman ever in the British Empire to hold the position of police magistrate. That had to count for something.

It did. She agreed.

Judge Emily Murphy presiding in Juvenile Court, 1918.

Photo Courtesy Glenbow Archives NC-6-3152

chapter two

The Day the Persons Debate Began

"People still speak of womanhood as if it were a disease."
   - Nellie McClung, 1916

One summer's day in 1916, Emily Murphy sat down behind a desk in Edmonton's courthouse, feeling decidedly overwhelmed and underprepared. She'd been studying laws relating to women and children ever since the Attorney General announced her appointment, she'd made notes and studied cases, she'd written for advice to her lawyer brothers in Ontario, but she was still very aware she had no formal legal training. This was a job she'd have to learn on the job, and she hoped the books she had piled on her desk would help. But, as it turned out, it wasn't the legislation that tripped her up. It was the British North America Act. In other words, it was the Canadian constitution.

One of the lawyers on that very first day challenged her right to preside over the court, any court, on the basis that she was not a "person" according to the BNA Act. Therefore, since she wasn't a "person" in law, she couldn't sit in judgment over his client.

There should have been cameras in the courtroom that day when Eardley Jackson told Emily Murphy she was not a person. Imagine the temerity! Why, just moments before, someone in the courtroom had called the newly ordained judge "Your Majesty." From "Your Majesty" to "non-person" was a bit extreme.

Of course, Emily Murphy carried on with the case as if she'd never heard the preposterous suggestion made by the lawyer. But that night, she checked on the BNA Act and discovered, to her horror, that indeed women were not consistently defined as "persons" in the nation's constitution. In matters relating to running for public office and voting in federal elections, the ambiguity had been cleared up by an act of Parliament. MPs had simply voted to allow women the right to vote and take office, but somehow the rules about appointment to the Senate had never been cleaned up.

Section 24 contained the troublesome words. It said: "The Governor General shall, from Time to Time, in the Queen's name, by instrument under the Great Seal of Canada, summon qualified Persons to the Senate, and subject to the Provisions of this Act, every Person so summoned shall become and be a Member of the Senate and a Senator."

"Qualified persons" had always meant "male persons." So it was that Emily Murphy heard again and again about Section 24 of the BNA Act and how she wasn't a person who could be a senator. Therefore, what made her think she could be a judge? "He was a poor fellow indeed who could not put up a new aspect of the argument," she wrote later.

As to the male lawyer who started it all, she had this to say in a letter she wrote to him October 25, 1917, about a year into her job. It is addressed to E.E.A.H. Jackson, Esq.:

> Sir, I am informed this morning in the Women's Police Court at the conclusion of the case of Rex vs Nora H., you in the presence of several persons, made use of the following grossly insulting words, "To Hell With Women Magistrates. This country is going to the dogs because of them. I would commit suicide before I would pass a sentence like that."
>
> Unless I receive from you an unqualified apology in writing, I shall regretfully be obliged to henceforth refuse you admittance to this Court in the capacity of Counsel.
>
> I have the honour to be, Sir, Your obedient servant, Emily Murphy, Police Magistrate for the City of Edmonton

No apology has been found among Emily Murphy's papers, but there must have been one because it is said that the lawyer Eardley Jackson relented on the matter of women magistrates, at least as far as Emily Murphy was concerned.

When Alice Jamieson was appointed a magistrate in Calgary, Alberta, she too had to endure the same tired "person" argument. In fact, one Calgary lawyer was so determined that a woman should not sit on the bench that he appealed one of Jamieson's decisions to the highest division of the provincial court where fortunately Mr. Justice Stuart took a sensible approach to the matter and declared that "reason and good sense" dictated that women could be judges. Thus, as far as the province was concerned, women were persons. That happened in 1917.

chapter three

The Passing Parade in Emily's Courtroom

The new magistrate soon learned that her law books did not anticipate the sort of human complications that came her way. How was she supposed to judge and, if possible, make better situations like the following? The first sign of trouble is in a letter written by Emily Murphy on October 26, 1917, to Mr. C. who lived in central Alberta:

Dear Sir,

Mr. and Mrs. H. of this city (Edmonton) consulted me recently about your wife who is here in the city and about to be confined. Although very heavy with child and in a highly nervous condition, she has been working in their home as a domestic servant.

I later had a conversation with your wife and advised her not to enter a suit for non-support but to effect a reconciliation if possible for your mutual benefit. She expressed her willingness to do this if you would agree to treat her more kindly and generously in the future. It seems a pity to create any unnecessary scandal or to bring you in here on a summons as defendant, thus running up a bill of costs against you, if it is at all possible to arrange the matter amicably.

I would therefore ask you to be good enough to come into the city upon receipt of this, that I may discuss it with you, and that some arrangement may be arrived at in the interest of both yourselves and your children.

Mrs. C. is not able to work any longer and is under my direct care. It is plainly your duty to protect your wife and unborn child at this time instead of leaving them to be a charge upon public charity. I cannot for a moment suppose that any man of your years of experience would be willfully guilty of so gross a dereliction of duty, and of so cold and unfeeling an attitude. I shall, therefore, expect to see you at the earliest possible date.

I have the honour to be, Your obedient servant, Emily Murphy, Police Magistrate for the Province of Alberta.

Mr. C. did not come into Edmonton, nor did he effect a reconciliation after that first letter. Emily Murphy had to write another, this one repeating Mrs. C.'s offer to come home…if he'd be nicer to her and help her with the five, soon to be six, children.

Most women knew they were "persons" in the common usage of the word. Who else but a person was looking after all those children and all those responsibilities?

Photo Courtesy National Archives of Canada C30784

20

Also, Judge Murphy emphasized, he must promise to buy his wife a new coat – she hadn't had one in nine years – and a set of teeth. It seems she had only two teeth left in front and Emily suggested as diplomatically as possible that two teeth were something short of a mouthful.

There are several other letters in the file from lawyers and social service agencies, all of them trying to solve the marital woes of Mr. and Mrs. C., all of them ending up on Judge Murphy's desk. How anyone could sort through such a tangled tale is hard to imagine, but that was the kind of case that Emily saw time and time again. Unhappy women in unhappy situations, some of them patently unfair, many of them involving the rights of women within marriage. Even though Mrs. C. didn't always please Mr. C., for instance, she was his wife. She had certain rights, but those rights had to be reinforced by law. Thus, dower provisions begun in 1911 in Alberta were amended and adjusted, inch by inch, first with the Married Women's Home Protection Act in 1915 and then the Dower Act in 1916. The first gave a woman the right to file a caveat to prevent the sale or mortgage of her home without her knowledge or permission. The second gave wives the right to live on the "homestead," the domicile shared during marriage as long as she lived. It also provided that any disposition of the land made without the wife's written consent was null and void.

There wasn't a similar flurry of interest in the Dower Act until the 1960s and 1970s when for the first time, the word "half" crept into the laws. Half of property and assets acquired throughout a marriage should belong to the wife, the new laws said, should there be a separation or divorce. Mrs. C. would never believe that such a law could happen. It was so far from her experience and the experience of women generally in the first few years of our social history in western Canada.

She might even have had some teeth. Maybe she could have added her voice to those who were urging the appointment of Emily Murphy to the Senate.

chapter four

If Women Weren't Persons, They Were Certainly Human

Emily Murphy was a doer. If a certain social problem presented itself time and time again, she'd try to figure out a solution, which is why she decided at one point that automobiles should be declared "public places" within the meaning of the criminal code. Otherwise, they were simply "moving houses of prostitution," she argued. Get rid of the "house," she argued, and young girls would not be so easily lured to their ruin.

The trouble was that girls and women continued to be lured to their ruin with all the attendant heartache that came with it in those days. This is the real story of Marion – the name is changed but the story is not. The first letter was written by Emily Murphy to Marion's father on May 21, 1917:

> Dear Sir,
>
> On May 19, your daughter Marion Thompson appeared before me in the Women's Police Court charged with vagrancy under clause 238 of the Criminal Code. She was arrested by Detectives Potheram and Appleby of the City Police Force at 12:20 Saturday morning, the 19th, in room 5 of the Petrograd Hotel…with Mr. George M., a real estate agent living in the Muttart Block. He is a married man. They were in bed. The book produced in court showed they had registered as Mr. and Mrs. Henderson of Calgary. They came in a taxi cab and brought no luggage.

After arrest and after being warned, Marion stated that she had been leading this life for three months having been drawn into it by the man to whom she was engaged. I found her guilty and remanded her to the care of Mrs. Askew, the matron of the Social Service Home, 11905-94 Street, Edmonton, until May 28 at 10 o'clock when she will appear for sentencing. Owing to her youth and to the fact that she has been out of work and that she has not been well, it is my intention to suspend sentence pending her good behavior. I also wished to communicate to you as her father that you might take the necessary steps to prevent her continuing the life she has been thoughtlessly and innocently drawn into. I hope you may not think hardly of her. If you think it advisable to let Marion remain at the Social Service Home for a period under the influence of the fine Christian influence of Mrs. Askew, you may do so by the payment of her board which amounts to fifty cents a day.

In this event, I shall commit her indeterminately. Her board for the next eight days will be paid by the Attorney General's Department unless you wish to pay it yourself. Unless you have some definite work under your own supervision, I would strongly advise this course, this being the turning point in her life. She is too good a child to lose to the white slave traffic and we must do all in our power to save her.

Kindly let me hear from you by return mail or by a night lettergram that I may know how to proceed.

I may say that we have not allowed her name to be put in any of the papers. She was represented by Jackson of Cormack and Mackie, Barristers of Edmonton. She requested him not to make the matter of her trouble known to you, and he spoke to me concerning her wish but I decided it was in her best interests to acquaint you with the circumstances.

I have the honour to be, Your Obedient Servant, Emily Murphy

P.S. Since writing the foregoing, I have learned from the matron of the Social Services Home that Marion

has been pregnant for three months. She has
confessed this but, as yet, has not been questioned as
to her child's father as she is greatly upset and very
nervous. She is now resting quietly at the home. I am
endeavoring to locate where she roomed and where
her clothing is.

May I assure you that this unfortunate child will
receive the best care and attention possible pending
instructions from you.

Marion's dad responds three days later and begins his letter to
Emily, Dear Sir:

Yours of May 21st received today re Marion. I must
thank you very much for your kind consideration
regarding her case. I myself could have done nothing
more. I would ask Your Worship to be kind enough to
let her go on suspended sentence on the grounds that
she report weekly to Mrs. Askew.

I am very sorry to learn the state of affairs and am
writing Marion and think that I can persuade her to
lead a different life in the future. If there is any cost
that is not covered by the Attorney General's
Department, please let me know.

Emily is not quite sure that Marion's dad has the whole picture.
On May 26, she writes him again:

Your letter of recent date received. I should be
pleased to act upon your suggestion if any
arrangement had been made for Marion's
maintenance but it would be wrong to turn her on
the street without a home or without work. Indeed,
she is not in a position to take work.

A certain man in town, I am informed, offered to
pay her fine if such is imposed which would lead me
to believe that she would be hopelessly lost if turned
adrift. Mrs. Askew left last night for a month's absence
in the East. She says that Marion has been threatening
to run away from the home and has not been
altogether amenable. Marion received a letter from
her mother but Mrs. Askew did not think she was

replying in the proper spirit.

Marion refuses to tell who the father of her child is which shows she is trying to shield him. For this and the reasons stated above, I would like to hear from you again. I will remand her further in the meanwhile.

I might say that Marion could go to the Beulah Home here for her confinement and if advisable, I could probably arrange to have the child made a ward of the Court and adopted into some good home, but this is some months away, the immediate problem being the placing her in some home in the meanwhile. It is just possible that some lady might take her in for light domestic work or the care of children.

Regretting that I have not been able to act entirely on your suggestion, I have the honour to remain, Your Obedient Servant, Emily Murphy, Police Magistrate

The next player to weigh in is Mrs. Thompson, stepmother to Marion. On May 29, she writes:

First, Madam, let us thank you for your kind consideration. I am sure it appears to the public as if we were very careless in regards to Marion. Not so. Marion has always been uncontrollable. She was 13 when she came to me as I am only her stepmother, and I always had trouble with Marion in this way. She was headstrong and self-willed. I tried, my sister tried to reason and talk to her. We were flatly told to "mind our own business." When I appealed to her father, she would say, "Why, daddy, I did not, I would not do such a thing. You can trust me, daddy." Not a month ago, she wrote her father the same.

Now, it seems almost hopeless. Her father received a very unsatisfactory letter yesterday, flatly refusing to give the name of the father of her child. No expression of sorrow whatever. Evidently she is trying to screen the man and I should suggest he is a married man when she is so determined. Would it be this M. or would it be some married man in the Hudson's Bay as she worked there until sometime in January? I also think that Marion must be at least four or five months pregnant. In February, she wrote me that she had been ill since Christmas. I wrote her at once to come home but she would not.

We are not situated financially to stand much expense but will do all we can. If the Home will take her for $10 a month, I will try myself to save this much. The child, of course, could be placed in a home. If her condition is so, she could hardly get a place for light housework and could not be trusted. As I can plainly see, Christian Influence is the only thing will ever reform Marion. She said the father of her child was willing to pay her expenses, but why can't she tell who it is?

I will do what I can for the poor child as she is a very bright girl and is a sweet little girl too, but very self-willed. I will pay $10 a month but would like to see her have some work to do. Light housework would be good for her physically.

I wrote Marion a letter yesterday that I think ought to touch her heart. If she still persists in being stubborn, it is almost a hopeless case. Probably the lady at the Home may have more influence over her than I.

Thanking you for your kindness, I am, Yours very truly, Mrs. W.T. Thompson

Apparently, Marion isn't completely hopeless yet for she writes to her stepmother and confesses everything. Then her father tells Emily Murphy:

Mrs. Thompson had a letter from Marion written May 30. She seemed very penitent and anxious to do what was right. I am glad Marion has told the name of the man who got her in trouble. In the letter she wrote, she said she was intoxicated. If it was this man who gave her the liquor, I think he could be punished under section 216 of the Criminal Code of Canada. If he is worthless and has no money, it would be useless to take him under civil action but if he was made to realize that he could be taken under the Criminal Code, he would likely bear the expenses rather than be arrested. If I were in Edmonton myself to talk to

him, I think that I could convince him that he is
criminally liable as she is under 18 and was lured
away from the guardianship where I left her.

If he will pay a certain amount every month, I
would like to place Marion away from all temptations
where she would get religious instruction daily as that
is the only thing will ever reform her now. Such a
place as the Beulah Home would almost be the best. I
cannot express how thankful I am to you for taking
such an interest in my poor child, but a lady as police
magistrate explains all.

I am, Yours very truly, W.T. Thompson

There's no more mention of Marion in Emily Murphy's files
until Marion herself weighs in with this letter two years later. She
writes from an Ontario address. How she got there is not
mentioned, but she has obviously not forgotten Edmonton:

Dear Mrs. Murphy, Received your letter and I do not
know how to thank you for your kindness to me. You
have been so awfully good to me. It certainly relieves
my mind to a certain extent. But oh, I am so
lonesome for my baby. I know she is in a good home
and I am so glad the probation officers visit the
home. They will see that she is well cared for but still
even knowing that does not keep me from wanting
her. Oh, how I wish I had never given her up. I know I
never will have another happy hour in my life. She is
constantly on my mind. My cousin who lives next
door is just my age and she is married and has a
lovely baby girl and it just breaks my heart to see her
with the baby. Never advise a girl to give up her baby
as I'm sure every girl's life is ruined when she loses
her baby.

I must close, again thanking you very much for your
kindness to me, and if you hear any more about little
Margaret, will you let me know?

Yours gratefully, Marion Thompson

There's such heartbreak in those few lines, and yet Marion could
not have kept her illegitimate baby in those days and kept her
place in polite society. That's just how it was, and Emily Murphy

had to sentence and advise accordingly.

It's no wonder she became the unofficial expert on social problems for other jurisdictions across Canada. You wanted to establish a policy on illegitimate children? Write Emily Murphy for suggestions. How should alimony be determined? Ask the woman judge. How to improve the lot of female prisoners? Ask Emily Murphy. She was everywhere and never hesitated to wade in where angels fear to tread.

Of course she got herself into hot water now and then.

When Emily saw that women's work was not protected by law, she began work on the Dower Act.

Photo Courtesy Glenbow Archives
NA-1320-5

chapter five

The Black Candle and Eugenics

As if she didn't have enough to do what with helping "fallen" women and wayward girls, heading up the Federated Women's Institutes, belonging to most women's organizations and keeping up with the demands of a family, Emily decided to write another book. This time, she would use her own name – no more Janey Canuck – and she would tackle a subject that would not sell. Her other books sold well in that they were lighthearted commentary about people she met, books she had read, places she had visited. But this one would be about the largely awful and ignored subject of drug addiction in Canada. How's that for a switch? Like most middle class women and men of her time, she hadn't even realized there was a problem with drugs in Canada but once she became a judge and saw the lives of girls and women ruined forever because of opium or cocaine, she decided to speak up. The book that resulted was called *The Black Candle*, published 1922.

In speaking up, she did four things: she revealed that drugs did exist in Canada; she revealed the degradation that addiction brought, especially to women; she tried to suggest some solutions, and she pointed fingers at the culprits. It's that last part that makes modern readers uncomfortable because she pointed fingers mostly at the Chinese population of Canada and she's not always kind in her condemnation. She also includes African Americans, Germans, Japanese and even Anglo-Saxons in her list of culprits, but the Chinese get the bulk of her blame.

She wasn't alone in this thinking, however. She wrote to police chiefs, government officials, social service agencies and judicial officials in Canada, the US and England and most of them, in responding to her questions about the extent of drug traffic and the possible cures, mention the Chinese race as the people who brought opium to the new world. She wasn't wrong in this thinking either. The Chinese did bring opium with them. Sometimes it was the only comfort they had in the alien situations they faced in new worlds. Unfortunately, a drug habit has to be supported, and that's how it became a problem in parts of Canada. And that's what Emily Murphy was writing about. It was a ground-breaking book. No one else had tackled the problems of drug addiction. Certainly, no one had noticed the degree to which women and children were affected, but Emily couldn't help but notice it. It came walking into her courtroom. She wrote about it as she saw and researched it.

It was her words that got her into trouble – not in 1922 when the book came out because everyone talked like that then – but in the late 1990s when no one talked like that anymore. She spoke of the "fertile yellow races," the "prolific Russians," and over and over again "the Chinaman." Sometimes she imitated the Chinese way of speaking. For a modern reader, it just won't do. But keep reading. When she gets to her conclusions, she doesn't let anyone off the hook, including her own ruling Anglo-Saxon race.

> In any study of the problems presented by the drug traffic, the relation of the girl pedlar to the yellow man is one which cannot be overlooked, and indeed it seldom is. Usually, we shift the responsibility for her fall upon the shoulders of the alien where it does not necessarily belong.
>
> Certain journalists, with all sincerity of purpose, have stirred up racial hatred against the Chinamen on this account, and have called them beasts and yellow dogs.
>
> Let us punish these foreign immigrants if they deserve it; let us exclude them from our country if our policy so impels, but let us refrain from making them the eternal scapegoats for the sins of ourselves or of our children. It is not the Saxon way.

The Black Candle wasn't exactly a best seller. After all, who wants to read about misery and hopelessness and government policies that need to be put in place? The book was intended for policy makers and governments, and that's where it went. The man and woman on the street didn't pay much attention. But they did pay attention to what Emily Murphy wrote about eugenics.

And therein lies another bone of contention.

The term "eugenics" came from the studies of one Francis Galton, a cousin of Charles Darwin, who produced evidence that "outstanding" individuals got that way through heredity. He first used the term in 1883. As a result of his research, he advocated the improvement of the human race through better breeding. Other international scientists took up the cause, discussed the idea at scientific gatherings and thus gave the whole idea intellectual credibility. Because it was a "scientific" development, it must be alright. Science was the new god then. It could even solve social problems, and a number of European nations adopted various forms of "eugenics."

Ironically, the Canadian who led this campaign to apply scientific solutions to social problems was a Methodist churchman, James S. Woodsworth, superintendent of All People's Mission in Winnipeg. When the first waves of immigration hit Winnipeg, he preached assimilation. Turn newcomers into good Anglo-Saxon Christians, in other words. When that didn't always work, he came out with a study called *Strangers Within Our Gates*, 1909, that abandoned some of his nobler ideas. Some immigrants were of "inferior stock," he wrote, and if Canada wasn't careful, the inferior stock would lower the intellectual and moral standards of Canadians in general. Therefore, he said, don't let the bad ones into the country, and if they're already here, then they may have to be prevented from making more of their own kind.

To be fair, the immigration problem was a complex one. There weren't simple answers for a population that changed with every boatload from another country. The Chinese immigrants were different from the Russians who were different from the Irish and so on. Canada was a melting pot that boiled over now and then.

It was an incredible time in our history, and neither science nor social gospel was able to fully comprehend and deal with the problem.

Woodsworth was distracted from his immigration complaints by World War One, during which time he became a pacifist and preached against violence of any kind. In 1919, he took part in the Winnipeg strike, and in 1921, became an Member of Parliament and served as such until his death in

In 1922 and under her own name, Emily Murphy wrote **The Black Candle,** *a book about the alarming drug trade in Canada.*

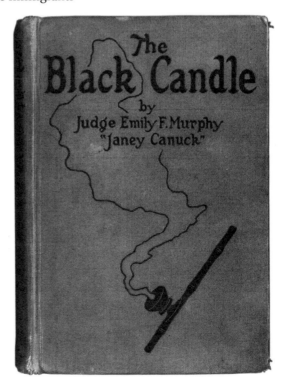

1942. In the 1930s, he helped found and lead the Co-operative Commonwealth Federation, the CCF, the socialist party now known as the New Democratic Party. Somehow, his earlier theories about segregation and sterilization were forgotten and forgiven.

Emily Murphy, however, didn't see how the other half lived until she became magistrate in 1916. Day after day in her courtroom, she saw women who had more children than they could care for, who had been abandoned, who had no money, who had no hope. Day after day, she dealt with children who were orphaned, neglected, or sold into prostitution. Many of the most miserable cases seemed a result of mental deficiencies. If mental deficiencies can be passed on from generation to generation, as the science of eugenics claimed, then it might be necessary to prevent certain individuals from creating more of their own kind. There'd be less crime, less abuse, less misery in the world if mental problems were thinned out. That was the message of eugenics and that was the line that Emily Murphy took.

The United Farm Women of Alberta were also intent on improving the human race. In a 1922 resolution to the United Farmers of Alberta, they suggested a plan "whereby the adult mental defective of both sexes be kept under custodial care during the entire period of reproduction." Four years later, they submitted another resolution that urged the UFA government to impose an act whereby..."if procreation is inadvisable, it shall be lawful for the surgeons to perform such operations for the prevention of procreation."

The Act Respecting Sexual Sterilization was passed by the UFA government in Alberta in 1928, and the Eugenics Board for the Province of Alberta was created. Between 1929 and 1972 when the act was finally repealed, a total of 2,822 men and women were sterilized in Alberta.

Emily Murphy wrote magazine articles in favour of sterilization. She couldn't have known how awful that would sound many years later but she was a woman of her time and lived within her social context. In the late 1920s, that included eugenics. She did not tie the need for sterilization to any one race. She saw it as a way of preventing the problems that come along with mental deficiencies. There weren't the social safety nets that we have now – social assistance, universal health care, addiction programs, birth control. Life, especially for women, was a gamble. If sterilization could better the odds for a decent life, then Emily figured it made sense.

Historian Anne White of Calgary said of Emily and others who supported the insupportable, "The demand that they (Emily Murphy and others) possess a fully integrated liberal view according to our modern interpretation is unreasonable. These women were in the process of changing society; that society was therefore in a state of flux as it evolved from one set of cultural standards to another. Society adapted and within that process the female reformers also changed and developed. It is wrong to criticize the women for not meeting our standards today as our standards have developed out of the reforms they initiated."

Women worked inside and outside the home, or, as Emily Murphy said, "Here in the wide and tolerant West, Everyone knows that a woman's boots are not pinned to her skirts.".
Photo Courtesy Glenbow Archives
NA-3017-4

chapter six

Back at the BNA Act

By the early 1920s, Emily was so well known for her social activism that a number of organizations forwarded her name to Ottawa as an eminently suitable candidate for the Senate. Time to have a woman, they were saying, and the first woman should be Emily Murphy.

As Emily said herself, "Here in the wide and tolerant West, everyone knows that a woman's boots are not pinned to her skirts." In other words, a western woman would be a dandy choice for Senate since they were strong, no-nonsense, able to carry their share of the load and then some.

But the dreaded words uttered on her first day in court came back to haunt her, this time from the federal government: women are not persons as defined by Section 24 of the BNA Act, therefore not eligible to be senators. Five administrations, three prime ministers said that between 1920 and 1927. Emily Murphy was thoroughly sick of the whole issue, she who did the work of five persons and took all the guff besides. And it made her even madder to know that the Members of Parliament might have initiated new legislation concerning the appointment of senators, but for some reason or other, they chose not to study the matter to see how it might be done. No matter how carefully she worded her letters of protest, no matter how many Members of Parliament made how many promises to change the law, the matter was not resolved. Apparently, there was just no way Emily could aspire to the Senate; she wasn't person enough.

Thanks to one of her lawyer brothers in Ontario, she finally found a way. He happened to be reading the Supreme Court of Canada Act and came upon a little known provision that said any five persons acting as a unit could petition the Supreme Court for an interpretation of any part of the constitution. What's more, the costs of the appeal would be covered by the Federal Department of Justice if it were judged to be of sufficient national importance.

Eureka. Two birds with one stone, both the way to challenge the law and the means by which to pay for it. That's when Emily Murphy began writing the letters that her daughter typed for her, and that's why her daughter says it was Mostly Mom.

This is the letter dated August 5, 1927, that first went to the other four appellants:

> Enclosed you will find a copy of Section 60 of the Supreme Court Act of Canada with also a letter to the Governor General in Council, which letter I am asking you to be good enough to sign and return to me by registered mail as soon as possible.
>
> You will recall that the National Council of Women, the Women's Institutes, the Women's Church Temperance Union, University clubs and other of our organizations, in convention, submitted resolutions to the Honorable, the Prime Minister at Ottawa, requesting of him that women be admitted to the Senate of Canada, thus permitting us to secure our full enfranchisement.
>
> As a result, with the approval of the Federal Cabinet, on June 25, 1923, in the printed "Orders of the Day," a motion was submitted by the Hon. Senator McCoig of Chatham, Ont., asking the members of the Upper Chamber that an address might be presented to His Most Excellent Majesty, the King, praying that he might be graciously pleased to give his consent to the submission of a measure to the Parliament of the United Kingdom to amend the British North America Act, 1867, so that "a female person shall be deemed qualified to be summoned to the Senate if she has reached the full age of thirty years and is either a natural born subject of the King, or a subject of the King naturalized under the provisions of any Act of the Parliament of Great Britain, or of any British Dominion or possession or of the Parliament of Canada."
>
> When this motion was read in the Canadian Senate, the Honorable Senator McCoig failed to speak to his motion; neither did he appear to speak upon the

same at any subsequent day when it was called so that the motion was never discussed. Since then, this motion has not been placed before the House.

As four years have since elapsed, and as it is now held by a large and important body of opinion that such proposed amendment was not, and is not necessary, it has therefore become highly desirable that this matter be determined without further delay in order that the women of this Dominion – comprising approximately one half of the electorate – may enjoy their full political rights on the same terms as these are, or may be, enjoyed by men.

It may here be pointed out that while in 1923, women generally were gratified in having Senator McCoig's motion placed before the Senate of Canada, with a possible prospect of its being later submitted to the House of Commons for added appeal to His Majesty, we have now come to realize that the matter is one which cannot with any degree of fairness be submitted for decision to a body of male persons, many of whom have expressed themselves towards it in a manner that is distinctly hostile. Undoubtedly, our proper procedure under these circumstances is to take advantage of a friendly recourse to the Supreme Court of Canada as provided for in Section 60 of the Supreme Court Act.

As the matter referred to in our letter to the Governor-General is purely a technical one, I have not thought it necessary to submit the matter to Canadian women generally, they having already endorsed the principle, but only to the few "interested persons" as specifically required by the Act, these being all from the Province of Alberta and women reasonably capable of giving an account of the principles that actuate them should they be required so to do.

I do not feel it even remotely necessary to urge upon you the extreme desirability of your lending your much-valued influence to this matter which is so closely allied with the political, social and philanthropic interests of all Canadian Women.

Yours very sincerely, Emily F. Murphy

You can see why Emily Murphy was accused now and then of arrogance. In this letter to the four women whom she thinks are most deserving of her trust, she still describes them-to their face- as "reasonably capable." Still, all four showed up at her house at the end of August, 1927, ready to sign on whatever dotted line she put in front of them. They knew their old friend. She was a bit on the bossy side, granted, but she knew how to get things done. They'd take her lead on this one.

Premier Scott of Saskatchewan stated that he was in favour of extending the franchise to women but did not care to exact the necessary legislation until women asked for it.

Photo Courtesy Glenbow Archives NA-3818-13

chapter seven

When Emily Calls

Emily Murphy had called, and Emily Murphy must be obeyed, but as Irene Parlby stood on her front steps waiting for Walter to bring the car around, she felt the familiar tug-of-war between her home and her political activities. On this late summer day, her garden was at its most glorious – orange and yellow nasturtiums climbing every which way, red poppies, blue and purple delphinium, early asters, late calendulas – they were all there asking for appreciation and attention.

But no, this day she must once again do her duty and represent her constituency of rural women. The meeting in Edmonton would be interesting and worthwhile, she knew, for anything that Mrs. Murphy initiated was bound to be, but it would have been so nice to sit for a bit. Maybe weed that back patch and transplant some of the Shasta daisies that were threatening to take over the whole farmyard.

Never mind, she told herself, and straightened both her spine and her wide brimmed hat. Time enough for lollygagging when her duty was done.

Once on the train from Alix to Edmonton, she watched the countryside roll by. So different from India and England where she had grown up, but a country that suited her very well nevertheless. She liked to be in on the beginning of things. That's what she had told her surprised mother and father back in England when she announced she intended to marry Walter Parlby and live on a farm in the North West Territories of Canada.

And even though her part of the North West Territories was now known as the province of Alberta, and even though there were roads now and trains and other amenities that she had fought for as an Alberta MLA, she still liked the newness of the place. The chance to make a difference.

What would it be this time?

Meanwhile, on the train from Calgary to Edmonton, Nellie McClung was not relaxing with a good book or simply enjoying the passing scenery. She couldn't. There were too many people who recognized her and wanted to talk to her about her books or about their troubles. One woman wanted advice about jobs in the city for her daughter. Another congratulated her for sticking to her guns about the prohibition of liquor. "It's the devil's own work," the woman told her and Nellie nodded in agreement.

It was only as they approached Edmonton that Nellie had time to think about the meeting ahead of her. She and Emily had already fought more battles on behalf of good causes than she could name. Together, they were a formidable force and they knew it, but there had been a slowing down in the last few years. Nellie's hair was noticeably grayer since her loss in the previous year's provincial election, and Emily's rollicking walk was a little less cocksure. There had been a time when Nellie McClung could have

Nellie McClung, the politician with a hammer in one hand and a quip in the other.

been pope, if only she'd been male and Roman Catholic, and Emily could have been a Senator, if only she'd been male and Liberal. They were that popular, or so some of their admirers told them.

But time changes everything. In fact, just last week, one of Nellie's friends told her she was getting stout. Mind you, you're being "neat" about it, the friend said. Cold comfort, Nellie thought, so that very night at her Bible class, she demonstrated a new reducing exercise, one that required her to get down on the floor on her bottom and bump along from hip to hip. As usual, her audience loved her antics and for a minute, she forgot about her fears of growing old and losing her effectiveness as a leader in social movements.

And now Emily had a new project. Nellie couldn't wait.

Louise McKinney spent the morning before Emily Murphy's meeting at a meeting of her own – an organizational meeting for the WCTU, the Women's Christian Temperance Union. It seems that some of the branches north of Edmonton had faltered, losing both membership and direction. Such carelessness could not be allowed, and Louise said so in no uncertain terms. How could they do this, grow careless about their responsibilities especially now that prohibition had been repealed? Greater action was called for, not less. The cords in her neck stood out as she spoke with such conviction about the need to defeat the forces of demon rum.

The meeting ran according to schedule, tasks were assigned and there was no question but that they would be done. Mrs. McKinney had not organized 43 WCTU chapters in western Canada without knowing how to get things done. To conclude the meeting, she led the group in prayer. Help us rid the world, she prayed, of the evil force of alcohol. Bless our efforts. Open the eyes of unbelievers.

For lunch that day, she ordered a poached egg on dry toast with a side order of stewed tomatoes. That's what she had when she was at home in Claresholm, and she did appreciate regularity and order.

The taxi was right on time, which was a good thing. Otherwise Mrs. McKinney might have had to say a few words to the driver about the virtues of being on time, but as it was, she simply straightened her hat and took out a notebook in order to make a short list during the drive to south Edmonton. "Things to check with E.M.", she wrote at the top of the page.

Henrietta Muir Edwards came to Edmonton from her home in Fort Macleod two days early in order to get some research done in the Legislative library. She was a familiar figure there – a dumpy little lady who dressed for comfort, not for style. Many's the time she had told the young librarians that they shouldn't wear corsets, even if they were the latest style. They squeeze your organs, she'd say to them. It can't be good for your health.

The young women didn't listen to her fashion advice but they certainly listened to her legal advice. Henrietta knew more about the laws affecting women and children than most lawyers and some judges did. She had been the national convener of laws for the National Council of Women for years; she knew her stuff. And when she didn't, she found out, which is what she was doing the morning before Emily Murphy's tea party. What were the laws relating to the status of women when the BNA Act was passed in

Henrietta Muir Edwards, the expert in laws relating to women and children.
Photo Courtesy Glenbow Archives
NA-2607-1

1867 anyway? Were women "persons" then? And if they weren't "persons" then, could they be "persons" now?

It was all very confusing. There didn't seem to be a clear Yes or No to the question even though Henrietta would have roared with laughter if anyone had suggested she wasn't a person. Of course, she was a person, no matter what the laws did or did not say. All women were; everyone knew that. But if the law was unclear, if it could be used to demean women, then something had to be done, and by gum, Henrietta wanted to be in on it.

At noon, she walked back to her sister's house, changed into her good blue cotton dress instead of her good brown cotton dress and tied it around the middle. Good enough. Have you got a hat I could borrow, she asked her sister, and when one was found, stuck it on her head in spite of the fact it didn't match her good blue cotton dress. But what did it matter? She wasn't there to make a fashion statement. She was there to make a legal statement.

Meanwhile, back at the Murphy house, Emily was not dusting her living room or whipping up a cake. She had hired help to do that sort of thing but she was putting the finishing touches to the petition that she wanted the other four to sign. It had to be right. She had already tried several versions – some long, some short, some full of longwinded legal explanation, some almost abrupt. The one she held now seemed the best – polite but not whiney, no-nonsense but not rude.

Who would have thought that Emily Murphy – she who had worked so hard for her sex and for her country – would be denied "personhood?" It was too much, especially since it prevented her becoming a Senator. She would have liked to be a Senator – the honour, the fuss, the chance to be the first. But no, she wasn't a person, according to some misguided notion in the Constitution. Well, time to fix that little red wagon.

She chose an afternoon dress for the occasion and fussed a bit with her hair. She would have preferred to wear a hat; hats covered so many sins, but hats weren't worn by a hostess. Only guests got to wear them which was too bad because Emily loved hats, especially if they had a plume or two, a bit of braid perhaps, probably another reason why the Senate beckoned her so. She could wear hats with impunity in the Upper Chamber. That would be part of the job.

As she waited on the verandah for her friends, she didn't notice the sun shining on her flowerbeds or the leaves glistening on the huge trees in her backyard. Instead, she saw herself in the Senate, and other women too, but she saw herself as the "first."

"Come on, girls. Let's get this show on the road."

They did. The five Alberta women on Emily Murphy's verandah that sweet summer afternoon on August 27, 1927, signed a petition that asked first: "Is power vested in the Governor General of Canada, or the Parliament of Canada, or either of them, to appoint a female to the Senate of Canada?"

Secondly, they asked: "Is it constitutionally possible for the Parliament of Canada, under the provisions of the BNA Act, or otherwise, to make provision for the appointment of a female to the Senate of Canada?"

In other words, they did not ask whether they were persons or not. They deliberately avoided the use of that term. They just asked whether the Canadian government had the power to appoint a female to the Senate, and if it didn't, what might be done?

Two simple straightforward questions.

"God bless our Cause and confound our enemies," Nellie McClung said.

"For outpost duty is the duty for me." A study group in Fort Macleod asked Emily Murphy for her favorite motto. This is what she sent.

chapter eight

"A Matter of Amazement and Perturbation"

Nothing in politics is simple. The petition went first to a government department known as the Governor General in Council. From there, it went to the Department of Justice where various officials debated it and decided the Canadian government did *not* have the power to name women to the Senate, not according to the BNA Act at any rate. (It was their understanding that the matter would require a rewriting of that part of the BNA Act, and that would have to go through the Parliament in England, still the last word on the Canadian constitution.) Ernest Lapointe, the Minister of Justice, however, decided that "as an act of justice to the women of Canada," the matter should at least be referred to the Supreme Court of Canada. At that point, the wording of the petition was changed and Emily objected. This is part of the letter she wrote on November 9, 1927, to the Deputy Minister of Justice, W. Stuart Edwards, after she had received a copy of her amended petition:

> We respectfully beg to point out that the question referred to the Supreme Court... is not the one submitted by your petitioners either in word or in meaning and is, in consequence, a matter of amazement and perturbation to us.
>
> In framing their questions on constitution, your petitioners were not unmindful of the fact that the officers of the Crown had already expressed the opinion publicly, and to various delegations, that a female was not a "person" under the BNA Act and, for this, and other very excellent reasons, refrained from using the word "persons" in any of our questions. We

therefore reiterate that the citation as forwarded to the Supreme Court of Canada by your Order-in-Council is not our question, nor a correct interpretation thereof, and that accordingly it requires to be withdrawn.

The petitioners do also respectfully draw your attention to the omission from the Order-in-Council of the second question, which question arises out of the first, particularly in the event of a negative decision by the Supreme Court.

To avoid delay and also the contingency of having to again appeal on this matter to the Supreme Court, your petitioners, as so entitled, have further enlarged their enquiry by the submitting of a third question to His Excellency, the Governor General, for the consideration and adjudication of the Supreme Court of Canada.

It reads as follows: "If any statute be necessary to qualify a female to sit in the Senate of Canada, must this statute be enacted by the Imperial Parliament (the Parliament of England) or does power lie with the Parliament of Canada, or the Senate of Canada?"

Emily concluded this protest with some well oiled political phrases: "Your petitioners were gratified to have the assurance contained in the... minutes of the Privy Council that the Honourable the Minister 'considers that it would be an act of justice to the women of Canada to obtain the opinion of the Supreme Court of Canada upon the point.'"

But she couldn't resist a parting shot. "We can have no doubt concerning the kind intent and goodwill of the Honourable, the Minister of Justice, and that he, accordingly, will take the necessary procedure to refer these three important and well considered questions on constitution to the Supreme Court of Canada in their original wording and in their given order."

So much for kind intent and goodwill. The petition, as revised without Emily's say so or blessing, went forward to the Supreme Court of Canada asking, "Does the word 'persons' in Section 24 of the BNA Act include female persons?"

It was better than nothing, and more than likely the other four appellants comforted Emily Murphy with that argument. But she was mad and said so in a long letter to Nellie McClung on

December 2, 1927, in which she lashed out right, left and centre –
at politicians who voted party before principle, at women who
didn't dare offend their men and at Easterners who under
estimated their western sisters.

> I hear, though, that it has been a terrible shock to
> the Eastern women that five coal heavers and plough
> pushers from Alberta (Can anything good come out
> of Nazareth?) went over their heads to the Supreme
> Court without even saying, 'Please ma'am, can we do
> it?' We know now how to stir up interest in the East –
> just start it going ourselves.

Once the Department of Justice agreed that the matter was of
sufficient national interest to be debated under Section 60 of the
Supreme Court Act, the Famous Five could only watch and hope.
It was out of their hands and into the hands of government
departments. Thus when Newton W. Rowell, KC, of Ottawa was
selected to represent their case, all they could do was cheer for
him. Emily, of course, wrote a few letters and researched a few
precedents that he might use. To her fellow appellants, she wrote,
"I am greatly pleased that he has consented. We could not have
better counsel. His being a Liberal too does not seem to make of it
a political issue which it is not in any sense."

He was supported by another lawyer from Ottawa, G.C. Lindsay.
Alberta sent along moral support in that the Attorney General's
department asked Rowell to represent them as well.

The other side was argued by Lucien Cannon, Solicitor General
and former MNA from Quebec; Eugene LaFleur and Charles
Plaxton for the Attorney General of Canada; and Charles Lanctot
representing the Attorney General of Quebec.

The judges were Chief Justice Anglin, Justices Duff, Mignault,
Lamont and Smith.

The hearing took place March 14, 1928, in a room in the
Supreme Court Building in Ottawa, and it was a hearing, not a
trial. It was an exchange of paper and polite arguments; it was a
detailed examination of precedents and legal opinion. It was not
rowdy, noisy, tumultuous, nasty. There were no cameras, no
reporters scuttling around. None of the five appellants attended.
Emily Murphy sent her brothers to take notes for her, but she and
her four companions decided to stay away for fear their
attendance might distract from the serious intent of the inquiry.

The two sides, Rowell on behalf of the Alberta women and Cannon on behalf of the Attorney General's department, submitted their written arguments first. Rowell's was three pages long supported by a 33-page appendix listing relevant precedents and laws. The factum concluded with the statement, "The Petitioners submit that the question should be answered in the affirmative."

The other side had a 24-page Statement of the Case, a nine-page factum, a 65 page appendix and a separate 11-page factum from the Quebec Attorney General. The Statement of the Case concluded: "...the question ought, accordingly, to be answered in the negative."

Page count did not decide the issue but it did send out a signal. Right away, it was evident that the Attorney General's department had the bigger guns, and as it turned out, the better arguments, at least as far as the Canadian judges were concerned. Earnest in their intention to interpret the law, the five judges listened to and questioned both sides all day, then adjourned to do further study and reading, but in the end, they could not answer in the positive.

Chief Justice Anglin reported their decision on April 24, 1928. He read from a long and detailed document, explaining himself all the way, but finally he concluded that he was...."of the opinion that women are not eligible for appointment by the Governor General to the Senate of Canada under Section 24 of the British North America Act, 1867, because they are not 'qualified persons' within the meaning of that section. The question submitted, understood as above indicated, will, accordingly, be answered in the negative."

He was careful throughout his ruling to explain the niceties of law that led to this decision, to emphasize that the decision had no bearing on the capability or desirability of women serving in the Senate. It was the law, that's all. They had to abide by the law as it was written and as it was intended.

Mary Ellen Smith from British Columbia said, "The iron dropped into the souls of women in Canada when we heard that it took a man to decree that his mother was not a person."

"The world loves a peaceful man but gives way to a strenuous kicker."
- Emily Murphy

chapter nine

Mother Was Not A Person?

How could any reasonable person say a woman was not a person? It didn't make sense then and it doesn't make sense now but in actual fact, the argument had nothing to do with the "common" usage of the word person. It had to do with "common" law.

In 1867 when Canada formed a confederation of provinces and became more or less independent of Britain, we took British law as the basis for our own laws. That system of law was known as "common law," and according to common law at that time, women were defined as persons in matters of pain and penalty but not in matters of rights and privileges. Therefore, when the lawmakers in 1867 said "persons" in connection with any kind of privilege, they meant male persons. This is known in law as "original intent."

And that was pretty well the sum total of the Attorney General's argument, but it was a powerful one. You can't go around changing the original intention of the law or you'd have no law, the argument went. You have to interpret a law based on the social and legal context in which the law was framed.

On the other side of the argument, Rowell tackled the word "qualified" first. That should be the key word, he said. As long as a woman was qualified, she should be eligible for the job. It not only made sense; it was the just thing to do.

Rowell also argued that a later government bill called the British Interpretation Act had cleared up the confusion between male and female persons. It provided that in all government statutes, words referring to the masculine gender should also be taken to refer to the feminine.

His opponents said No, that act referred to a specific case. I didn't apply to Section 24. Besides, all the pronouns in and around the section on the Senate were "he" or "him" or "his," thus proving for once and for all that the original intent was to have male senators.

Rowell switched tactics and pointed out that in 1928 Canadian women could vote, hold public office, own property – none of which they could have done in 1867. In order to pass the Dominion Elections Act to give women the right to vote in federal elections, for example, the word "persons" in other sections of the BNA Act had been opened to mean both male and female persons. Why not the same treatment for Section 24? Otherwise, the BNA Act was inconsistent.

Never mind, the opposing lawyers said, the right to vote was enacted by the Canadian government. The government had simply passed legislation allowing women the vote. The government had not seen fit to do likewise with the Senate. Therefore, the rules had to be maintained as written. Even if the government wished to change the rules about qualified persons for the Senate, there might be problems because the Senate was a new creation. It was not based on the British model of the House of Lords in the same way as the House of Commons was based on its British predecessor. The common law defining women's legal incapacity to hold public office had to apply. All the more reason why women could not be senators.

"Besides, what real woman would want to dirty her hands with politics?" Nobody actually said those words out loud but they were definitely a subtext. There were lots of men and women who still believed that a woman's place was in the home; a man's place was everywhere else. Chief Justice Anglin tried to steer clear of the hidden agenda. He stuck to the common law and original intent arguments, and they won the day.

chapter ten

Best Letter Ever Written

They were so ladylike. Not a nasty word was leaked to the press after the decision was announced, not a single banner was unfurled in protest.

But Emily Murphy was not finished. While Parliament in Ottawa dithered during the spring session over whether to attempt an amendment to Section 24, she considered her options. And when the Members of Parliament went home for the summer of 1928 without changing anything, she quietly activated the next part of her plan – she would appeal to the Privy Council in England, still the highest court of appeal for Canada.

An appeal to the Privy Council was no small matter in 1928. Even the name "Privy Council" conjured up images of solemn bewigged judges in solemn far off places considering matters of huge national and international importance. Matters like, Who was to blame for the sinking of the Titanic, and How were all those pink parts on the map of the world to be properly governed? Hardly ever would you think of the Privy Council taking on something as seemingly mundane as "Are women persons?" And yet, that's what Emily Murphy decided to do.

This is how she explained her decision to her four co-appellants in a letter dated May 2, 1928, one of the most masterful pieces of political and personal correctness you'll ever find, not to mention positive, uplifting and forgiving. This is part of what she wrote:

> Enclosed you will find an appeal which I have addressed to His Excellency, the Governor General in Council, asking that our Reference in regard to the meaning of "Persons" under Section 24 of the B.N.A. Act, 1867, be referred on appeal to the Judicial Committee of the Privy Council.
>
> Be it understood that this appeal must not be

construed as in anywise expressing a lack of
confidence in the determination of the Honourable,
the Minister of Justice, and his colleagues of the
Cabinet to devise means whereby the B.N.A. Act may
be amended to permit of women sitting in the Senate
of Canada, but only that we, as Petitioners, can have
no certainty that the exigencies of politics or the
dissent of one or more of the provinces may not
preclude the possibility of such amendment....

While we regret that the decision of the Supreme
Court of Canada was not favourable to our cause, I
am sure we are agreed that their decision was a
sincere one and should not be adversely criticized by
any of us.

For the several years past, the Women of Canada,
owing to what appeared to be a hopeless situation,
took comparatively little interest in this matter of the
interpretation of the word "Persons" in Section 24 of
the B.N.A. Act. Our action in appealing to the
Supreme Court of Canada for a ruling gave to the
women of all parties a renewed hope and had the
effect of stimulating them to something approaching
definite action. We have every reason to felicitate
ourselves in this behalf.

Of the ultimate results, I have not the slightest
doubt. Nothing can prevent our winning. Every editor
in Canada except those of Quebec is backing us in the
appeal. When the time is ripe, it can reasonably be
predicted that the French Editors will also concede in
the justice and propriety of our claim.

It is also truly encouraging – and we may take the
assurance to our hearts – that no extension of the
franchise has ever been defeated since John, the King
of England, signed the Magna Carta at Runnymead.

She wasn't nearly as confident as she sounds in this letter and
she admitted as much in a letter to Rowell. "If we lose in the Privy
Council, we are still as far ahead in achieving our ends, in that the
Federal government has pledged itself to these." (To finding ways
to amend the constitution.)

And speaking of moving ahead, Premier Louis Taschereau
decided that Quebec would not contest the appeal in London as

they had done in Ottawa. Not that he had changed his mind as he made clear in a letter to Emily Murphy:

> Although I believe that the great majority of the women of Quebec do not want the franchise, nor the right to sit in parliament, it was only fair that we should leave the determination of the legal aspect of the matter to the Privy Council without interfering.

Emily Murphy was delighted. Her careful letters were paying off, and once more the government agreed to pay the costs of the appeal.

She continued her careful path through the political minefields when she decided *not* to go to London to sit in on the hearing. In another letter to her four cohorts, she explained, "I had thought of attending this appeal in London, indeed had intended to, but upon maturer consideration thought it would only prejudice our cause."

Thus, on July 22, 1929, when the hearing began in a room at #1 Downing Street, there were no Canadian women present. Several women from suffragist organizations in England were there as interested spectators but otherwise the event was a men-only event. The British judges were Lords Sankey, Darling, Merrivale, Tomlin and Sir Lancelot Sanderson. The lawyers for the five appellants from Alberta were N. W. Rowell and Frank Gahan. The lawyers there to uphold the Canadian decision were Eugene Lafleur, Geoffrey Lawrence and Theobald Mathew. The lone provincial representative was J.F. Lymburn, Attorney General for Alberta.

Like the Canadian hearing, the appeal was mainly an exchange of paper and precedents in law – very little emotion or fireworks. Terribly polite, terribly proper. It was emphasized by one and all that the whole issue had nothing to do with the ability or the right of women to serve in public office. It was an interpretation of the law that was being sought. To that end, both sides remained formal and stiff-upper-lip.

A Canadian Press reporter wrote about the hearing:

> It is all very orderly and dignified. Everyone is very polite. Mr. Rowell makes a statement or reads long excerpts from the B.N.A. Act. Lord Merrivale, ponderous and very wise looking, asks a question and Mr. Rowell replies in many words. Deep and intricate

questions of constitutional law are debated back and forth. The exact shading of meaning to be placed on certain words is argued to the finest point.

   And so on it went for four long days at the end of which time, judgment was reserved. Lord Sankey would announce the decision in the fullness of time.

Lord Chancellor Sankey arriving with the verdict.
Photo Courtesy Glenbow Archives
NA-4953-1

chapter eleven

Thousands of Words Later

Finally, on October 18, 1929, Lord Sankey sat before a crowded courtoom in London and read and read and read, and although there were clues along the way as to the final decision, it wasn't until he had read every word of the 20-page document that he finally made it clear. This is his one sentence conclusion, a sentence that reveals the complexity of the material throughout the report:

> A heavy burden lies on an appellant who seeks to set aside a unanimous judgment of the Supreme Court, and this Board will only set aside such a decision after convincing argument and anxious consideration, but having regard: (1) To the object of the Act – namely, to provide a constitution for Canada, a responsible and developing State; (2) that the word "person" is ambiguous, and may include members of either sex; (3) that there are sections in the Act above referred to which show that in some cases the word "person" must include females; (4) that in some sections the words "male persons" are expressly used when it is desired to confine the matter in issue to males; and (5) to the provisions of the Interpretation Act; their Lordships have come to the conclusion that the word "persons" in s. 24 includes members both of the male and female sex, and that, therefore, the question propounded by the Governor General should be answered in the affirmative, and that women are eligible to be summoned to and become members of the Senate of Canada, and they will humbly advise His Majesty accordingly.

In other words, Yes. Yes, women are persons in the B.N.A. Act and can therefore be appointed to the Senate. It is reported that Emily Murphy heard the news in the middle of the night and danced around in her flannelette nightie saying, "We've won, we've won."

So how did the higher court come to their decision? Tortuously, that's how. Read the 20-page decision and you're snowed under by all the fine points of law concerning the meaning of persons, the intent of common law, the various acts that led to the formation of Canada under the BNA Act, the significance of other laws that touch upon all of the above, and so on. It would not make good television, this oh-so-careful legal analysis, but somehow, out of the wilderness of words and opinions came a clear message. It was almost magic.

To begin with, Lord Sankey named all the appellants, the five women from Alberta, and briefly outlined their contributions to Canadian life. The fact that there were five honest-to-goodness "persons" behind the petition gave it life, anchored it to real people instead of turning it into a law lecture as had happened in Canada.

Then he tackled the business of "common law." It's true, he said, women were still under a disability to run for or hold public office in 1867 when the BNA Act was passed to create the confederation of Canada. There were still vestiges of the old argument that women were "persons" in matters of pain and penalty but not in rights and privileges. However and however, he said:

> The exclusion of women from all public offices is a relic of days more barbarous than ours, but it must be remembered that the necessity of the times often forced on man customs which in later years were not necessary. Customs are apt to develop into traditions which are stronger than law and remain unchallenged long after the reasons for them have disappeared. The appeal to history therefore in this particular matter is not conclusive.

To the argument that all the pronouns used in connection with the Senate were masculine pronouns – he, him and his – Sankey said, "The British North America Act planted in Canada a living tree capable of growth and expansion within its natural limits." In other words, things change.

"I believe that never was a country better adapted to produce a great race of women than this Canada of ours, nor a race of women better adapted to make a great country."
- Emily Murphy

57

Emily must have burst her buttons when she read those words. So many of them echoed her own. She could have been forgiven the occasional, "I knew it. I said so. I told you so." There is no official record of such outbursts, however. The judge in England used his words carefully. The judge in Edmonton did likewise.

Lord Sankey's final argument cut through all the long words and convoluted legalities. "The word 'persons,'" he read from the legal decision, "may include members of both sexes, and to those who ask why the word should include female, the obvious answer is why should it not? In these circumstances, the burden is upon those who deny that the word includes women to make their case."

The Persons Case made front page headlines.

Photo Courtesy Glenbow Archives
NA-3813-12

chapter twelve

Yes, Yes and Yes Again

The Persons Case was reported in most Canadian newspapers but since most women thought they were persons already, it was not the biggest news item ever. Only those who had been fighting the good fight for women's rights for so long understood what a major accomplishment this was. The very day that she became a person, Isabella Scott of Montreal, for example, sat down and wrote Nellie McClung a letter that jumped off the page with excitement and congratulation:

> I am so thrilled tonight that I do not know if I can write a decent letter. O, the joy of being a person, a qualified person…think of it. Nothing so important and far reaching has happened since that famous convention in the sixth century where it was decided that women had souls. I understand it was a Christian affair…If this dear Canada of ours was not such a big country, the right thing to do would be to have you five brave women from Alberta come down here and join in the hurrahs. You have certainly covered yourselves with glory and your names should go down in the history of Canada as the liberators of your sex.

Emily Murphy may have wanted to make some grand pronouncements but she didn't. When a reporter asked her if the "persons decision" represented a victory over men, she answered carefully, "We, and the women of Canada whom we had the high honour to represent, are not considering the pronouncement as standing for a sex victory, but rather as one which will permit our saying 'we' instead of 'you' in affairs of State." Who could argue with that?

"She who would put on gloves must learn to spar."
- Emily Murphy

The same kind of restraint was evident at the party held at the Palliser Hotel in Calgary soon after the Privy Council announcement. The five women who signed the petition were there, and they must have enjoyed the tributes and stirring words that came their way but they never crossed the line into "I guess we showed them." Always ladylike, always diplomatic. In order to add her words of wisdom to the gathering, Henrietta Muir Edwards, the shortest of the five, had to climb up on a chair to make herself heard and seen over the crowd and din of the room. Obviously, there was some celebrating going on even if the Famous Five downplayed their part in the Persons Case.

At a luncheon for the Women's Canadian Club a few months later, all five spoke again. Emily emphasized that action must follow words. It's not enough to be persons, she said, we must "dip down and drink," meaning that women must get involved. Irene Parlby echoed those sentiments. If women take a share in politics, she said, every legislature in Canada will be filled with women. Louise McKinney got a laugh when she addressed her audience as "fellow persons" and then advised the women to "develop honour, justice and everything that is big." Henrietta Muir Edwards urged the audience to give credit where credit is due. Many men helped along the way, she reminded them. Don't forget that the government paid for both appeals. And finally, Nellie McClung brought down the house when she said she had always wanted to be a person. In fact, she had always had an instinctive feeling that she was one, she said, tongue in cheek.

And when the celebrations were finished and men and women went back to their regular lives, the one thing they knew was that it would only be a matter of time before Emily Murphy, Alberta's own, would be named to the Senate. Canada's first female senator. It had to be. And to be honest, Emily wanted it more than anything else she'd set her cap for. Deep down, she knew she'd be good. Deep down, she knew she deserved it and so did the women who supported her and needed her. After all, she had been immersed in women's issues for years. Who else had traveled through the countryside hearing tales that would curl your hair about conditions for women? Who else had seen them come before her day after day in the courtroom? Who else had written so many letters that her files spilled out of boxes and piles both at home and at the courthouse? Who else had belonged to so many women's organizations that her entry in *Who's Who* was three pages long?

She waited for the call. It had to come.

chapter thirteen

No, No and No Again

But there's more than one way to keep a good woman down even if she is a person. You can name someone else as the first female senator, that's what you can do, and that's what the federal government did four months after the Privy Council decision. They picked Cairine Wilson, a well-connected Liberal from Ontario, a worthy choice in every way except that she wasn't Emily Murphy. It was a horrible slap in the face for Emily. She wanted that job. She earned that job. She should have had that job.

As if that wasn't bad enough, rumours began circulating about a quota for women in the Senate. Maybe one was enough? Maybe five? This is what Emily had to say to her friend and ally Nellie McClung about that:

> Now, this looks suspicious to me in view of the fact that both parties are out wildly to see how they can amend the BNA Act. Even those gentry who said they'd stand "no tampering" with it. They can only tamper when it suits their personal or political ends. Now all these politicians, without exception, are bursting with wrath and it looks to me as if they are trying to get the two parties (males, of course) to join up on restricting female "persons" to five, and if we don't keep our sharpest weather eye open, the BNA Act will be amended in Canada so that only five "persons" or at best one from each province can sit in the Senate.

The handwriting in this letter gets bigger and bigger as Emily gets madder and madder about the whole situation, and by the time she mentions the newspaper accounts of Cairine Wilson's first day in the Senate, she is almost apoplectic. Apparently, Wilson was ushered into the Chamber on the arm of Senator

Dandurand, his sword shining at his side, her gown trailing daintily behind her. Emily wrote:

> I'd like to take a shot too at the Opening... Isn't it time that both swords and trailing gowns be put out of the Senate? Senator Dandurand's sword caught in Senator Wilson's train much, we are told, to the amusement of the onlookers. I can't see either why she should have been "supported" on his arm while going up to be sworn in. She went there as an equal and not as a supported or protected person. At the same time, the Senators refused to stand or cheer. They were absolutely right in this. We want no pretty dainty "perfect ladies" such as the Gazette admires and we must watch out that unsuspecting (or even catty females) don't fall into this attitude of mind.

Even at the end of this six-page epistle, Emily can't quite leave go of the bone. She squeezes in at the bottom of the page:

> I see that some Montreal women are saying "Quebec as the first province" should have had the first woman Senator but the editor of the Montreal Herald reviewing her letter seemed to favour Alberta next. Ah well, no one loves us now. It's nothing for us but the "garden" and "worms," and worms I can see.

It wasn't like Emily to worry about death, at least not out loud. She was only 62 years old. Lots of time yet to be a senator and whatever else she wanted. But as she waited for the call, she wilted. Personal problems were never discussed in those days but Emily Murphy had diabetes and sometimes it showed.

In 1931, Emily Murphy resigned as police magistrate and juvenile court judge for Edmonton, retaining the titles on a provincial basis only. Theoretically, she should have had more time for herself but she couldn't refuse requests for speeches, magazine articles, favours. One month she's quoted in the newspapers telling a Lions Club to "Frown on war, ridicule it, never sanction it. If there is another war, don't let yourself be stampeded into joining in. It is better to die fighting against it than to die fighting in it." Such strong words for a woman to be saying at an all male meeting, but Emily never could resist a challenge. In Montreal, speaking to the Women's Club, she told them that "We want women leaders today as never before, leaders who are not afraid of being called names and who are willing to go out and fight. I think women can save civilization."

For awhile, Emily could say just about anything and tread on toes everywhere. If only she could have had that blasted title. But 1932 passed without a nod from Ottawa.

And in 1933, she died. Went to bed one night and didn't wake up. She was only 65. The doctors guessed it was heart trouble brought on by the diabetes but there were others who said her heart finally broke, she was that disappointed.

William Arthur Deacon of the Toronto Mail and Empire wrote the most loving obituary: "I think she was the heartiest person I ever knew. The West was the place for her expansive spirit." About the missed Senate seat, he said, "I often thought she was wasted hearing theft cases. Her proper place was in the Senate where her intelligence might have functioned to wider purposes. And fancy Emily Murphy's laughter in the Senate! Perhaps that was what the politicians who kept her out really feared."

Nellie McClung immediately wrote a tribute:

> Certainly there was nothing maudlin or weak about her ruling, nothing hesitant or indefinite. But there always was a kindness in her sternness. She hated wrongdoing but she was always sympathetic and anxious to win the wrongdoer to a better way of living. No one knows how many wayward girls were set on the straight path by her kindly motherly ministrations.

Helen Weir, an old friend who aided Emily in her crusading days, remembered the Persons Case:

> In life and death she proved she was a person. All her life she fought for the finer things of life, not for herself for she already had them, but for the other people; and she died like a person, in full possession of her faculties until the last. There was no withering of beauty or brain, no falling of the leaves, no winter of decay, no cry for help, just a quiet passage from the light of earth to the glory of heaven. She was never old. She lived like a person and died like a person.

chapter fourteen

Happy Most of the Time

Emily Murphy had so many titles, so many honours. How could she possibly care about one more? And yet she did, and she deserved it. Nobody worked harder, nobody stayed up later, nobody tackled more worthy causes than she did. She was often wrong, misguided, rude, a busybody, but she was involved. She was present in her time. She should have had that job in the Senate. It wasn't fair. A Greek tragedy played on the western plains.

It may have given her some comfort that her name was connected to just about every other worthy cause in Canada. It may also have helped her to get letters like this one from the Methodist Parsonage in Thornloe, New Ontario, April 17, 1922:

> I am taking this liberty of writing you because I feel you are one of "God's Great Souls" who are trying to lift Humanity to a higher plane. I am just one of the lesser lights who feel a great love for God and desire to make this world a better place for my having lived, and so I find myself engaged in this great work with my husband. Our Ladies Auxiliary are making a "Comforter" and I would love to have your name (and subscription, if possible) for that Comforter. I have the centre worked with the names of Missionaries who have worked in this north country and have just one space left on one block that have Premier Drury's and Mrs. Drury's name on. Then as the block takes four names, I have Mrs. Nellie McClung's name and if you would consent would be delighted to have yours written in the other corner. If I have taken too great a liberty, I trust you will pardon me, but my knowledge of your life and work leads me

to believe in you and seek your kindness. Yours for service, Maud Moddle

Emily wrote back saying, Go ahead, use my name, here's my money, and thanks for the kind words.

But obviously the kind words weren't quite enough. She wanted the title. In a letter found in her papers after she had died, she wrote: "I want you all to remember at this time that I had a fairly long and fairly full life, and that I was happy most of the time – happier than I deserved."

There's more than a little bit of regret there.

There's also a parting word to her granddaughter, another Emily. "Tell Emily Doris she is to take up my work and carry it on when she grows up. She's in training for it right now, only she must be better and stronger than me."

Who could live up to such an impossible task – to be better and stronger than the original Emily? Certainly the young Emily Doris was not up to it; she lived a quiet life and said very little about her famous grandmother. In fact, her daughter, Emily's great granddaughter, admitted she knew next to nothing about the first Emily. End of conversation. End of line.

Alberta didn't get a female senator until 1979 when Prime Minister Joe Clark appointed Martha Bielish from Warspite. Why it took so long is a puzzle. Maybe it's pure coincidence and political maneuvering but by the same token, maybe it's a compliment to Emily. Emily was one of a kind. Emily couldn't be replaced – not for a very long time anyway.

Let's leave it at that. Rest In Peace, Emily.

chapter fifteen

Henrietta Muir Edwards, First To Sign

"I do not mind in the least being called old so long as I am not classified as an antique."
- Henrietta Muir Edwards

Emily Murphy was the ringleader; she was the Famous One. The Persons Case would not have happened without her, not in 1929 at least. But she needed the support of the other four Alberta women who signed the petition with her. They too made significant contributions to the history of the west and Canada generally. They were Henrietta Muir Edwards, Nellie McClung, Irene Parlby and Louise McKinney.

The remarkable life of Henrietta Muir Edwards began in the Victorian era when men were men and women were not. It ended in the 1930s when men were still men but women were persons. It was an amazing transition experienced by an amazing person!

Born in 1849, she was the oldest of the Famous Five, the daughter of a privileged Montreal family, someone who might have been expected to settle down inside four safe walls after finishing school and the obligatory tour of Europe. Instead of that, she talked her father into buying a big house in downtown Montreal where she established the Working Girls Association, a Young Womens Christian Association (YWCA) forerunner where single girls could get rooms, job training and legal advice. It was all quite remarkable. Well-to-do daughters didn't usually meddle in social reform in those days, but Henrietta was an evangelical Christian who believed in practising what was preached. For her that meant social action.

Marriage didn't change her mind about the work God intended her to do. It just made it harder since her doctor husband Oliver Edwards moved all the time. In 1883, he moved to Indian Head in the North West Territories as official doctor for Indian reservations in the area. While there, Henrietta did what she could and what she must – she wrote letters to family and fellow activists, she studied Canadian law, and she looked after the children – Alice, Muir and Margaret.

In 1890, it was back to Ottawa for a spell. Without pausing for breath, Henrietta joined forces with Lady Aberdeen, the wife of the Governor General, and helped her establish the National Council of Women, the Victorian Order of Nurses and the YWCA. The Governor General's lady was in a marvelous position to initiate things because she traveled constantly with her husband across Canada, but it was people like Henrietta who organized the follow-up and wrote the necessary bylaws and constant letters. That was Henrietta's role – continuing care, the grinding backroom work.

The National Council of Women followed her wherever she went. They needed her for her growing knowledge of law as it related to women and children; she needed it to keep in touch with other women and places, especially when Oliver moved west again, this time to the Blood Reserve in southern Alberta.

Henrietta Muir Edwards as a young wife and mother with husband, Dr. O.C. Edwards, son Muir, daughters Margaret and Alice.

Photo Courtesy Glenbow Archives
NA-4035-164

The National Council of Women was a pyramid organization that operated on three levels: the national level, the provincial and the local. The national level was an umbrella for all provincial and local groups. The local groups were in turn umbrellas for all other women's organizations in the area, the theory being that every woman in Canada could have her say through the Council of Women, and with such wide representation, the governments would have to listen. That was the theory anyway and most of the time it was so. The Calgary Local Council of Women, for example, in its early years included some 48 affiliates from women's church groups, the Women's Christian Temperance Union (WCTU), the YWCA, the Women's Canadian Club, the Women's Press Club and so on. When they presented petitions to the local aldermen, they got a hearing because they represented so many votes. They didn't always get what they wanted but they were a force to be reckoned with. The same was true on the national stage. For many years, the National Council of Women was so powerful that its members were guaranteed an annual meeting with the federal Cabinet, the only women's organization that ever got that concession. Part of the reason for its strength was Henrietta Muir Edwards who was the National Convener of Laws.

An older Henrietta in 1921.
Photo Courtesy Glenbow Archives
NA-4035-124

It was she who had to know the laws of the country. If the members of the WCTU wanted the vote for women, for example, they would make a resolution at the local level. The local executive would pass that on to the provincial body which would pass it on to the national which would then write Henrietta and say, "Check it out and tell us what to do."

The process was cumbersome and slow, but Henrietta always came through with a resolution that could be forwarded to the appropriate level of government. In the end, she knew Canadian law concerning women and children so well that lawyers and judges asked her for advice, not the other way around.

And there never seemed to be any conflict between her religion and her political activities. It was principle she was interested in, and if the principle involved justice for women, then it had to be God's will. If that made her a feminist, so be it. She didn't divide things into male and female. Instead she spoke of being "co-workers with God." This is how she concluded a speech in 1906: "And so standing in the yoke of God, co-workers with Him, let us find rest in our work, the rest He gives in labour, working with Him in the great battle of good against evil, of right against wrong."

The speech incidentally was a warning against the seduction of luxury. Don't spend too much money, she told her Local Council of Women audience:

> There is another phase of this subject even more culpable than extravagance in cost and that is the absolute slavery to fashion under which so many of us groan: a dress, a hat, a coat perfectly good in every way is discarded simply because it is last year's style... So many hours are spent in shopping, and exhausting conferences with dressmakers are held, all because fashion has ordered that sleeves must be no longer full at the wrist but full above the elbow. How far removed is such conduct from the actions of reasonable beings. What a simple waste of time, money and energy.

That's Henrietta for you. Her granddaughter admitted years later that her grandmother had practised exactly what she preached in the above speech. Somewhere along the line, she had decided that corsets could not be good for the body, squeezing the organs as they did, so she stopped wearing them. Consequently, her granddaughter said, she looked like a potato sack tied in the middle. Such independent thought was unusual in those days when to be a woman was to be bound up in whalebone and squeezed into a proper shape. Not Henrietta, however. Nor was Henrietta keen on hats, partly because Oliver didn't like them but also because they were a nuisance. She really didn't have time to worry about such unimportant things.

Nor did she have money. Henrietta, of all the Famous Five women, was the poorest. Oliver wasn't a particularly good provider, and Henrietta never got paid for any of her research or work on behalf of women and children. She did it because it had to be done. No more need be said.

In 1899, as Convener of Laws for NCW, she produced a major

summary of the laws in every province of Canada that related to the protection of women and children. Unfortunately, it was a short summary because there weren't nearly enough laws to protect either women or children. That's when Henrietta began her lifelong affair with property law. If God's justice is to be done on earth, then women must have a say, a stake, a share in the family property, both for their own benefit and for the benefit of the children.

It was a hard sell. Men hated to give up the absolute power they had over the buying, selling and willing away of their land. But Henrietta whittled away at it, sometimes alone, sometimes in concert with other women and other organizations. This is what she wrote to her daughter Alice from Edmonton in 1916:

> Yesterday I addressed a large emergency meeting called to consider the "Dower Act," now before the House. After it is passed, I will send you a copy. I have met quite a number of the members this session, the speaker several times. You will be pleased to know that my book on the Legal Status of Alberta Women has been well received and has received the approval of a number of lawyers. I will bring you a copy.

She doesn't always speak this formally to her family. In fact, she was a very loving mother. She wrote to Alice on September 12, 1926:

> Fifty years ago this evening, I was married. If Oliver had been here we would have been celebrating our golden wedding. It seems impossible that that day which does not seem so very far back was fifty years ago. In looking back, the way seems strewn with blessings, hard places there were sometimes in the road but what happy companionship! What a son! What two dear daughters! What a husband! I think few women are so blessed as I.
>
> I feel very grateful to God for I do not deserve what he has given me. My husband and I walked together in perfect accord for 39 years. My children have never given me any anxiety...I cannot tell you how grateful I am that I have you- such a dear daughter you have always been. I think it is wonderful that I cannot recall a single incident when you and I disagreed.

Such amazing grace. When she wrote this in 1926, her daughter Alice was the only one of her three children still living. Son Muir died of the flu in 1918 when he volunteered to work with flu victims in a temporary hospital at the University of Alberta, and daughter Margaret died in childbirth. Henrietta was living in reduced circumstances with her sister Amelia in Fort Macleod; yet she could rejoice.

When Emily Murphy approached her to take part in the Persons Appeal, she agreed at once. What else had her life been about? And due to the fact that the names of the five appellants were listed in alphabetical order, the case became known as Edwards vs. Attorney General of Canada, an unintended result that seems fair somehow. Henrietta spent so much time studying Canadian lawbooks, it seems right that her name be in them too.

She died in 1931, two years after the successful conclusion of the Persons Case. She was 82 years old.

Not many women went the route of these two who homesteaded land in their own names. At least their dower rights were never in question. Dower rights were a particular concern of Henrietta Muir Edwards.

Photo Courtesy Glenbow Archives
NA-206-27

chapter sixteen

Nellie McClung, Second On The List

Nellie McClung could hit you over the head with a hammer at one moment and then in the next moment tickle your funny bone. It was an unbeatable combination – this ability to rouse people to the need for reform, even uncomfortable reform, and then make it appealing.

On one occasion, she was told that women, angels that they were, were too sweet and frail to mingle in public life. "In that case, women should be rushed at all speed into public life," she retorted, "there being a decided shortage of angels in the field now."

In urging prohibition upon her audiences, she used to tell the story of the worms in gin. During a demonstration at a school one day, she dropped one worm into a glass of water and another into a glass of gin. The worm in water did just fine, but the one in the gin up and died. "What lesson does that teach us?" she asked the children brightly. "If you drink whiskey, you'll never get worms," said one of the students. It was a great story to warm up and disarm a hostile audience.

When people who had had enough of prohibition argued that moderate amounts of liquor were better than no amounts of liquor, Nellie McClung said that their argument put her in mind of Bernard Shaw who once declared that other planets must be using this one as their insane asylum.

Even the thirsty members of the audience could smile at that.

With her ability to make the medicine go down, Nellie McClung became the most popular of the Famous Five, the one best remembered. In fact, her own personal reputation outlived most of her causes, a fact that would have been regrettable but for the fact that Nellie McClung *was* her causes. Mention the vote for women and Nellie McClung's name springs to mind. Or

prohibition, or women in the church, or women in public life. Wherever women were, there was Nellie McClung.

Born October 20, 1873, in Chatsworth, Ontario, Nellie moved with her family to Manitoba in 1880, a transplant made necessary for all the usual reasons – a need for more land and opportunity for the six Mooney children. As a child, she was rambunctious and stubborn, qualities that were nourished by her father but discouraged by her stern mother.

Vowing to be different somehow, to be more than just a wife and mother, she took teacher's training, taught for several years and then became just what she had vowed to avoid. She married Wes McClung and started down the traditional path – wife, mother, club member. It was her mother-in-law who opened another door. "Let Alice do the washing," she told Nellie one day, knowing that Nellie wanted to enter a fiction contest. So the hired girl washed that day, and Nellie wrote her first short story. The

Nellie McClung somehow found time to write 15 books in between raising a family, fighting for the right to vote, prohibition and personhood.

Photo Courtesy Glenbow Archives
NA-1641-1

story didn't win but it became the first chapter of her very successful novel, *Sowing Seeds in Danny*.

By today's standards, the story is too sentimental for words, but it was a bestseller then and Nellie McClung's name became a household word.

The senior Mrs. McClung was also responsible for Nellie's introduction to public speaking with an invitation to speak about her newly released book to the local chapter of the Women's Christian Temperance Union. The speech was a great success and from then on, the die was cast. Nellie McClung realized she could write and speak, and what's more, she had a mind to do it.

When the family moved from Manitou to Winnipeg in 1911, Nellie shifted into high gear. She joined the Canadian Women's Press Club and through their social programs toured local factories in an effort to understand wage structures and working conditions as they applied to the predominately female working classes. Her horror at what she found in the sweatshops was reinforced by the views of Emmeline Pankhurst and Barbara Wiley, prominent British suffragettes who visited Winnipeg and gave stirring encouragement to the local budding suffragettes. More and more, Nellie McClung realized that the laws protecting the weakest members of society – women and children – were woefully inadequate.

Because the WCTU was also involved with making a better world, Nellie increased her activities in that area. Always, she worked within her church. Even though she wasn't always as stern as her Methodist mother would have preferred, nor as silent as her long suffering Methodist ministers would have liked, she turned up every Sunday to teach Sunday School, to debate with the minister after the service, to comfort the afflicted and afflict the comfortable.

It was an exciting time to be alive. Nellie and her colleagues were so convinced of the rightness of their causes that nothing could dissuade them. Besides, they had religion with them. To be a good woman at the turn of the century was to be a good Christian woman. To be a good Christian woman was to believe that the world could be made perfect if only Christianity was lived in all its fullness. If God be with you, who can be against you?

Who, indeed? In 1914, Nellie wrote her only non-fiction book, an angry tirade called *In Times Like These*. It was a stinging indictment of government, church, society and men, but even that was accepted with fairly good grace. The world was not always the

"The hand that rocks the cradle rules the world is a beautiful fiction, handed out to soothe us when we are restless. The hand that rocks the cradle does not rule the world or many things would be different."
- Nellie McClung

best of all possible places, so criticism seemed a reasonable response, especially when it came from a woman who could make you smile as you squirmed.

There's no doubt she was at the top of her form, in that lovely space that exists before doubts creep in. As she admitted in her autobiography, "There was a queer streak of cheerful imbecility in me up to a certain point in my life... I used to say that if anyone wanted to hurt my feelings, they would have to submit their case in writing."

Thank goodness, she was such a cheerful imbecile. If she hadn't been, she might not have taken on the battle for universal suffrage and if she hadn't, there's no telling how long it would have taken the women of Canada to get the vote.

In Winnipeg, the Women's Political Equality League was formed with the enthusiastic support of Nellie McClung who became their chief spokesperson, travelling around the province persuading women to work for the vote. She'd stand up in front of the local WCTU or Ladies Aid group and talk about her five children, admitting that she and her husband had taught their youngest to tell visitors, "I am the child of a Suffragette and have never known a mother's love." That always got a laugh. Then she'd reassure the group that she'd brought some of her husband's socks to darn after the speech and, oh, by the way, women could make a better world if they had the right to vote. That was the ticket, that was the appeal of the vote. It would make a better world because women would, of course, vote the right way. They would vote for better schools and better hospitals and dower laws that protected innocent women and children. They would vote for the continued prohibition of alcohol and they would vote for peace. It would be a better world, just you wait and see!

It's not hard to understand the magic that the women's movement attributed to the right to vote. Simply, it meant the power to do good. It would give women power to change things and there were things that needed to be changed. The woman whose husband squandered his pay cheque on liquor knew for a fact that she could change that with the vote. The woman whose babies died in infancy knew she could elect people who would see that health services were improved. The woman who couldn't read knew that the vote would change that. The phrase, "When women have the vote…" preceded many a declaration of intent to make things better for all.

It wasn't hard to marshall women and women's groups to the

"Chivalry is a poor substitute for justice, if one cannot have both. Chivalry is something like the icing on cake, sweet but not nourishing."
- Nellie McClung

fight, especially when Nellie McClung was out front smoothing the way. It was somewhat harder to marshall the men to this point of view, especially one man, Manitoba Premier Rodmond Roblin. The most patronizing of men, he remained convinced that the whole issue would go away as soon as decent women heard from the decent men in their lives that they should go home and be quiet.

Women's place was in the home, he said, her duty the development of children and the management of a home. A newspaper headline described his position: Premier Roblin Says Home Will Be Ruined By Votes For Women... Children Will Be Left To The Servant Girls... Retrograde Step... Can See Nothing To Commend It. Even with a delegation of the most respectable women in front of him, Nellie included, he rumbled on about the bloom leaving the rose if the rose stoops to dabble in politics.

Writing about it later, Nellie said, "We went there asking for plain common justice, an old fashioned square deal, and in reply to that we got hat lifting. I feel that when a man offers hat lifting when we ask for justice, we should tell him to keep his hat right on. I will go further and say that we should tell him not only to keep his hat on but to pull it right down over his face."

That's when one of the Political Equality League members described a mock parliament that had been done in another city. Why don't we do the same thing, she asked, and why don't we have Nellie McClung for the part of the Premier? No sooner said than done, they booked the Walker Theatre in Winnipeg, listened very carefully to the arguments in the legislature as to why women should *not* be allowed to vote and then turned it into a debate on why *men* should *not* have the vote.

Not only that but they charged a fee for the privilege of attending this spoof, calling it theatre, and put some money in their club coffers. It was a masterful achievement in more ways than one.

Nellie as the Premier was wicked. Just as Roblin liked to spout cliches about women being too fair and fine for politics, she described men in the room as being such splendid physical specimens that they should never ever stoop to the dubious exercise of politics. Where Roblin argued that women were too emotional to vote effectively, Nellie suggested that men might be unsettled by voting. They might begin and never quit, and where would that leave jobs and family and friends?

To conclude the devastating lampoon, Nellie lowered her voice and said, "Perhaps the time will come when men may vote with women, but in the meantime, be of good cheer. Advocate and educate. We will try to the best of our ability to conduct the affairs of the province and prove worthy standard bearers of the good old flag of our grand old party which has often gone down to disgrace but never – Thank God – to defeat..."

She brought down the house.

Two years later on January 28, 1916, Manitoba became the first province in Canada to grant women the vote.

Nellie wasn't there to lead the victory parade because she lived in Edmonton by then, but she didn't miss all the excitement. In fact, she was in Alberta in time for the historic assault on the Legislative chambers on February 27, 1915. Premier A.L. Sifton had agreed to meet a small delegation of women before the afternoon sitting but without his realizing it, small groups of women had been drifting into the public galleries and then onto the floor of the legislature until the place was jammed with women. What could he do? Call the police? Think of the newspaper headlines. So he and five other cabinet members had to sit and listen, for a change.

Henrietta Muir Edwards was there from Fort Macleod. She asked that the last bar against universal suffrage – sex – be removed.

To celebrate getting the vote in 1916, Nellie McClung, Alice Jamieson and Emily Murphy did the most rash thing they could think of – they had their pictures taken.
Photo Courtesy BC Provincial Archives

Alice Jamieson, judge from Calgary, said "Why not give us what is ours without having to beg for it?" And Nellie McClung, the newest Albertan but not the newest politician said: "We hope... you are not going to tell us women do not want the vote and therefore should not get it. Many things which women did not want in the past have been thrust upon them- the present war, the liquor traffic, unequal pay for equal work. There may be some women who do not want the vote, but surely you would not want the irresponsible women to set the pace for the rest of us."

"Mrs. McClung and Mrs. Murphy are very determined women," the premier told the press later. Sure enough, a year later, April 19, 1916, the bill giving Alberta women the right to vote in provincial elections was passed, making Alberta the third province to give women the vote. (Saskatchewan beat Alberta by a month. Their suffrage bill was passed March 14, 1916.)

Judge Alice Jamieson was in Edmonton the day that women were granted the franchise, so she called up her friends Emily

The Grain Growers Guide,
July 8, 1914

Photo Courtesy Glenbow Archives
NA-3818-14

THE VOTE GIRL

I WANT THE VOTE, AND I MEAN TO HAVE THE VOTE; THATS THE SORT OF GIRL I AM

Murphy and Nellie McClung. We should celebrate, she said. "Being women," said Mrs. Jamieson later, "we couldn't very well express our joy and satisfaction by going out and getting a bottle, so as we walked down Jasper Avenue with our arms interlocked, Mrs. Murphy suggested that the most rash thing we could do would be to have our pictures taken."

1916 was a big year for women in Alberta. Emily Murphy became the first female police magistrate in the British Empire, she and Nellie McClung and many others campaigned for the right to vote and got it (although they didn't actually vote until 1917 when a provincial election was held) and biggest surprise of all – the province went dry. In a referendum held early in the year – before the franchise was extended to women – the male voters of Alberta voted to prohibit liquor.

Amazing. Women were saying, "If we could manage all of that without the vote, think of what we'll do with the vote." They were heady times.

Nellie McClung wrote to a Mrs. Reeve on April 10, 1919:

> I think this is the greatest and best country in all the world, with its great sunlit spaces and its long long roads, and best of all the roads that are not made yet, and the stories that no one has told because they are too busy living them. I like it because the people here have room to be themselves and are not so hedged about by conventions and precedents and traditions. These things do not bother us nor make us afraid. Neither have we very much respect for them for we make them ourselves. It is just like a homemade hat. It may be quite as nice as the one you buy but you haven't the same respect for it because you know how it was done. That's the way we feel about precedents.

Still on top of the world, Nellie McClung was elected to the Alberta legislature in 1921 as an Opposition MLA from the city of Edmonton for the Liberal party, not that the party mattered. Whenever an issue came up that affected women and children, she voted as she saw fit, often with Irene Parlby who sat on the other side of the House as a government member of the United Farmers of Alberta. Not that that mattered to her either. The pair of them worked quietly together on issues of health care, education, matrimonial property rights, child protection.

Nellie McClung and Emily Murphy worked together as well through the various organizations they both belonged to and at the "pink" teas that were the height of Edmonton society in those days. Nellie was a favourite at these social events; she'd leave them laughing. Emily sometimes did the opposite. One woman said years later, "She was a dreadful person. Never knew when to shut up. Always wanting us to do her work for her. And she wouldn't always wear gloves."

There you are – the ultimate social sin in the 1920s. Still, whether by honey or hammer, Nellie and Emily got things done, separately and together.

In 1924, prohibition was repealed. The voters of Alberta, including the female voters, cast their ballots to bring back a regulated sale of liquor. Nellie McClung was stunned. To think that her women, the ones she'd been talking to all these years, would betray her and themselves so badly. Hadn't she proven in her newspaper articles that jails had emptied, children were better fed and clothed, women weren't beaten and neglected? "Women could have sobered this country," she wrote bitterly, "if they had willed it so; that is a sore and withering thought. Why do we hold life so lightly? We, the women who pay for it with sweat, blood and tears? How can we be indifferent to the evils which mar our creation?"

As if she hadn't been hurt enough, she lost the 1926 election by 60 votes. 60 votes. Even though she was now a resident of Calgary, she expected the old magic would still be there. But her stand on prohibition wasn't much appreciated, and her zeal wasn't much needed. The world was going on without her and it hurt.

Then along came Emily Murphy with her "persons" petition in 1927. Of course, Nellie would sign. Here was an issue that went beyond specific concerns to matters of principle. If women didn't think they were persons, how could they stand up for their rights in other areas? How could they see their way to changing the world with the vote? And how could men, for that matter, change their attitudes as long as injustice still existed in law?

After 1929 and the successful outcome of the Persons Case, Nellie McClung continued to fight the good fight on as many fronts as she could handle, including the one which she supported loyally all her life – the church. Most particularly, she wanted to see women in the pulpit as fully ordained members of the clergy, but that was a hard sell. "The Church of Christ should have championed the woman's cause," she told an audience at an

international church conference in England. "It should have led all the reform forces in bringing liberty of soul and freedom of action to women... It is a sore thought that the church has let us fight our battle against social inequalities alone." And a few years later, when the Alberta government decided that women should be barred from bars, she couldn't resist another dig, "With the Senate doors open now, there are only two great institutions that will not accept women on equal terms – the church and the beer parlours."

In 1932, the McClungs retired to Victoria. The climate was gentler, the pace of life slower. Nellie took on the job of first woman on the CBC Board of Governors and true to form, she spoke up for women. First of all, more women than men listen to

Nellie McClung was the only member of the Famous Five who was able to attend the unveiling of the Senate plaque in Ottawa. She is on the far right, beside Prime Minister Mackenzie King.

Photo Courtesy Glenbow Archives
NA-3043-1

81

"I never could believe that minding one's own business was much of a virtue, but it's a fine excuse for doing nothing."
  - Nellie McClung

radio, she pointed out. Therefore, their needs should be considered when it comes to programming decisions. Then she told the corporation they should hire more women. That suggestion went over like a lead balloon, of course. One eastern Canadian newspaper sneered, "We'd like to hear one of them (ie women) handle a professional hockey game this winter." As if hockey games were the sum total of the CBC. Who would have thought social justice would be so difficult? Nellie McClung withdrew somewhat from the front lines and began writing her autobiographies, *Clearing in the West* and *The Stream Runs Fast.*

Nellie McClung might have accepted a Senate nomination had it been offered, but there's no record that it was offered. The Famous Five were to be permanently frozen out of the Senate for their temerity. The closest they came was in 1938 when they got their names on a plaque mounted in a hallway near the Senate chambers. On that occasion, there was an official ceremony and the women wore evening dresses and everything was very posh, but it was just ceremony, no more. Nellie McClung attended on behalf of the Famous Five, and seems to be saying in the pictures taken that day. How could this be – that I alone remember our glory days and am here as some relic of the past? Where have all the causes gone? All the earth-shaking changes we worked for?

Nellie died in 1951 at the age of 78. The words on her gravemarker in a Victoria, B.C., graveyard are "Loved and Remembered," an epitaph that is heartfelt, of course, but a bit on the abrupt side. Why not one of her favorite sayings, like: "Never retract, never explain, never apologize, get the thing done and let them howl."

chapter seventeen

Louise McKinney, Next To Sign

Louise McKinney was one of life's lucky ones. She knew what she had to do in this world and she never doubted for a minute that she'd be rewarded in the next. The Women's Christian Temperance Union, was her platform, her purpose, her life. Others may have dubbed the club, "Women Continually Torment Us" and others may have made sport of its determination to rid the world of liquor, but Louise knew it was the only way to go. It was the Christian way. The "C" in the name of the organization made all the difference, she used to say. God was with her.

That being the case, she and her fellow WCTU members waded in where angels feared to tread. They worked for prohibition, of course, because they could see all around them the results of too much alcohol – women and children who were neglected, abused, impoverished. It seemed so logical, so sensible, so Christian, to work for the elimination of the stuff.

But apparently the sale of liquor couldn't be stopped unless women had the vote, so the WCTU added its voice to the suffrage battles. There was no contradiction there; their vote would make the world a better place. So they sent resolution after resolution to the government; they wrote letters; they signed petitions; they joined delegations that called for change.

The first WCTU Convention ever held in Alberta was in 1904, and the resolutions set forth at that meeting set the tone for the WCTU ever after. The Resolutions Chairman was Louise McKinney.

> **Resolution #1:** Be it resolved that we acknowledge God as our leader in all things, and that we continue to recognize prayer and faith in Christ as the foundation principles of our work.

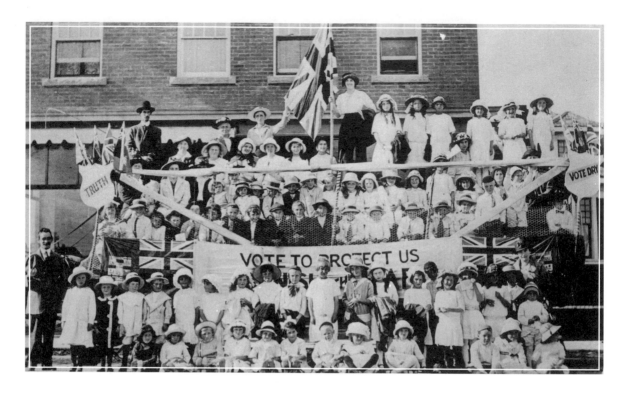

The WTCU pulled out all the stops in their fight to rid the world of alcohol. Here the children are used to get the message across – Vote to Protect US, Vote Dry.

Photo Courtesy Glenbow Archives
NA-1639-2

Resolution #2: That as an organization we urge that men and women everywhere shall practice and encourage total abstinence from alcoholic drinks, and in view of the fact that the liquor traffic is morally wrong and therefore can never be made legally right, we stand for the entire prohibition of its manufacture, sale and use.

Resolution #3: That we put forth the most strenuous efforts for the enforcement of the present law against the sale of cigarettes to minors; and also that we continue our efforts to induce the Dominion government to prohibit the sale, manufacture and importation of the same.

Resolution #4: That we guard our Lord's day, and that we cooperate with the Lord's Day Alliance in endeavoring to secure better observance of the same. That we do our best to assist trainmen in obtaining

Sabbath rest by discouraging Sunday travelling; and that we discourage Saturday night shopping and all other work which tends to prevent a proper observance of the Sabbath Day.

Resolution #5: That our women be urged to use the limited franchise we have and continue our efforts for the full enfranchisement of our sex, knowing that it is one of our strongest weapons in the battle for the reforms we are seeking.

Resolution #6: That we earnestly entreat the members of the WCTU to discourage by their example the use of bird plumage for millinery purposes, and that we encourage the formation of humane societies and bands of mercy.

The WCTU members at the provincial level combined religion and temperance and bird plumage and the vote all in the same pot, and then when they got back home again, they did whatever needed to be done in their own communities – libraries and health clinics and reading rooms. No job was too big nor too small for the WCTU. If it needed to be done in the name of Christian justice and love, then it was done.

It must have been fun to be a feminist in those early days. The task was so clear; no one could question the value of the work being undertaken. Not that the WCTU'ers called themselves feminists. They were "willing workers for the Cause;" they were "God's messengers on earth." Just because most of their concerns involved women didn't mean they were feminists. It meant they were Christians who wanted a fair shake for everybody, women included.

Born in 1868 in Frankville, Ontario, Louise Crummy joined one of the youth programs of the WCTU when she was still a school girl. At every meeting, she pledged: "I will never falter until this land is freed from the bonds of the distiller, brewer and government company." She learned to say things like, "Alcohol debauches manhood, debases womanhood, defrauds childhood," and learned to sing songs with titles like "Father's a Drunkard and Mother is Dead." Add that kind of pressure to a stern Methodist upbringing and you have some idea why Louise turned out to be the strong stern, directed woman she was.

Frances Willard, the founder of the WCTU in the United States, has to take some credit for Louise's strength as well. It was she who realized that women in the late 1800s could not be seen as militant or radical, so in order that club members might challenge the status quo without losing what they had, she came up with the impeccable slogan, "For God, Home and Native Land." Who could question such noble ideals?

Certainly not Louise. While teaching school in North Dakota, she became an organizer for the national WCTU and when James McKinney came courting, she saw in him a fellow worker for the cause. So they were married and produced a son whom they named Willard.

Many Americans moved north to Canada at the turn of the century in search of better land, greater opportunities, and so did the McKinneys. Louise was barely unpacked in their new home in Claresholm before she was out on the road talking up the need for a WCTU presence in western Canada. By 1912, she had 43 chapters going in Alberta and Saskatchewan. It was an incredible accomplishment but then she was an incredible woman. This is how her son Willard explained it: "She was patient and could wait for the purposes of God, but how she could drive slackers. She was truly tolerant of people – the last to condemn a sinner – but how she could flame in the condemnation of evil."

A Claresholm old-timer remembered those flames. He attended a prohibition rally when he was just a kid. Sitting up front right under the stage, he could see the cords on her neck stick out like timbers, he said, as she preached the evils of alcohol.

Mrs. Doris Stevens of Fort Macleod was a member of one of Mrs. McKinney's youth groups and to this day, she cannot look an alcoholic drink in the eye without suffering pangs of conscience, no matter how weak the brew or how refined the occasion.

The WCTU's finest hour occurred in 1915 when the citizens of Alberta voted for prohibition. (The vote was in 1915; the actual implementation didn't occur until 1916.) And the most exciting part of it all was that women didn't actually have the right to vote at the time of the referendum. That came later in 1916. But somehow they managed to influence enough men to vote for prohibition through their dedication, their arguments, their righteousness. If they could accomplish that without the vote, think of what they could do with the vote. Surely the world was going to be a better place.

In 1917, Louise McKinney quietly ran for the Alberta legislature,

WOMEN'S CHRISTIAN TEMPERANCE UNION

(White Ribboners)

The Second Public Annual Meeting of the above Society will be held (D.V.) in the

St. Paul's Methodist Church

12th Street, HILLHURST

ON FRIDAY, MARCH 6th, 1914

Speaker, DR. C. F. WARD, B.A.
Calgary University

Subject "IT"

Chair to be taken by Mrs. Harold Riley at 8 o'clock

Supported by
Mrs. Fred Langford, Prov. Vice Pres.
Mrs. Barbara Cassels, (Langdon) Dist. Supt.
Mrs. Grace Boyd, Prov. L.T. L. Sec'y.
Mrs. P. S. Woodhall, Pres. Central Union
Mrs. H. M. McCallum, Pres. West End Union
Mrs. Lebeau, Pres. Crescent Heights
Mrs. Roe, Pres. Hillhurst; Mrs. McElroy (Past) Pres.
Rev. W. P. Freeman, B.A., Rev. Peter Walker, Rev.
W. Hollingsworth.
SOLOS: DUETS, MRS. AND MISS McELROY

A VERY HEARTY INVITATION IS GIVEN TO ALL

(Red Cars)   COLLECTION

Alcohol was so despised that it couldn't be named in this advertisement. Alcohol is referred to as "IT".

Photo Courtesy Glenbow Archives NA-2629-19

quietly won, quietly became the first women to sit in a provincial legislature in the British Empire. A technical first since two women were elected that year but Mrs. McKinney was at the opening of the legislature that year while Roberta MacAdams was still overseas as a nursing sister. Therefore Louise is distinguished as the first to "sit."

Mostly, that's what she did – sit. Patiently, quietly, only opening up her considerable vocal cords whenever liquor or women's rights found their way onto the order papers . She was certainly behind the amendments to the Dower Act that passed through the House in her years there, but otherwise, she kept her counsel.

When the Canadian Home Journal asked her to write an article in 1919 on "Where Are Women Going?" she wrote:

> For answer, let us pause and ask another question. What, after all, is the purpose of woman's life? The purpose of woman's life is just the same as the purpose of man's life- that she may make the best possible contribution to the generation in which she is living.... Since many women will either from choice or from force of circumstances, continue to earn a living outside the home, are we not in duty bound to stand for the principle of equal pay for equal work?

Such radical talk for a woman who goes on to urge that women stay in close touch with God and the Church, and yet Louise McKinney saw no contradiction. Justice was justice.

In 1921, she ran again, again as an independent since she had heard that organized political parties accepted funds from liquor interests, and she would have none of that. However, the world was changing. The men who came back from the war were not too happy with the WCTU since they had opposed both tobacco and liquor for the service men. The boys who had served overseas had seen liquor used in what looked like pretty civilized ways in Europe. Maybe prohibition wasn't the only way to go. Maybe indeed education and moderation might work better.

And that's why prohibition was repealed in 1923. (Again, the vote was taken in 1923; alcohol was not actually back until 1924.) It was a stunning blow for Louise McKinney and the WCTU, not the least because women had the vote this time around and used it to Bring Back the Bottle. How could they? The vote was supposed to be used to build a Good Decent World. It wasn't supposed to be used for booze.

Left without prohibition or politics, Louise McKinney transferred some of her energy to the controversies surrounding the idea of church union. She was in favour and was the only western woman to sign the Basis of Union that created the United Church out of a combination of Methodist, Congregationalist and some Presbyterian churches. Besides that, she kept a closer eye on her community. In 1924, she wrote to Emily Murphy for advice concerning the troubles of a local woman:

> We have a case here that is rather distressing. There is a Mrs. S. of Norwegian parentage and I believe illegitimate birth. I understand also that her father

Louise McKinney and son Willard, grandson Norman. Willard was named after Frances Willard, the founder of the WCTU. (c. 1930)
Photo Courtesy Doris Haslam

was an uncle of the unmarried mother. At 17, this girl was married to Wm. S. She is now 36 and the mother of nine children of whom eight are living. They are on a farm near Claresholm and succeed in making a living somehow.

Mrs. S. is obviously below normal but her eccentricities are well known by the people about town and they simply smile and let it pass. During the years there have been two occasions when she fell from grace. At one time her husband accused her of improper relations with a man who kept a poolroom here in town and on another occasion she ran away with the hired man and was gone six months. Of late, she has been coming to town altogether too often and has made herself rather annoying by speaking to perfect strangers – either men or women – and by wandering about the streets. A few weeks ago, she noticed that several ladies were going in one direction so followed one group and attended a reception that one of our brides was holding that day – quite a stranger to her but she just wanted to go and it didn't cost anything. About that time there was a worthless fellow in town, who may or may not have himself been mentally deficient, but who, at any rate, saw in her a victim, so he induced her to spend the night

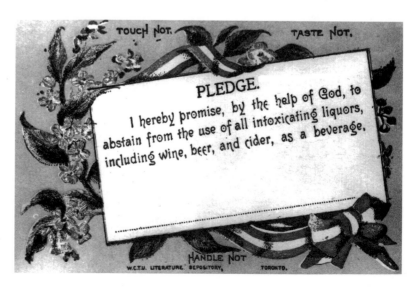

The pledge taken by all WCTU members urged the rest of the world to "Touch Not, Taste Not, Handle Not".

Photo Courtesy Glenbow Archives
NA-3199-1

with him in town. Which she did and altogether without money consideration.

Our policeman, who is rather an officious type of Englishman, had been watching her so he arrested her the following morning and brought her before the local magistrate. Her husband was present but was of course angry with her and refused to pay any fine in her behalf. Her mother who lives about two miles from her was not notified. There was no defense and no counsel for the accused and they sentenced her to six months in Fort Saskatchewan for being a common prostitute. The whole town is outraged, but what can we do? ...The man in the case was given two hours to get out of town while this poor creature is sentenced for six months in jail. Should one try to have the sentence shortened and if so, how could one proceed to do it?

Sincerely yours, Louise McKinney

Probably Emily Murphy advised her friend to get busy and advocate for what would today be called Legal Aid, and probably Louise McKinney did just that. There was no sense dithering. Louise McKinney was not a ditherer. Consequently, when Emily Murphy approached her to sign the Persons Petition, she did so without hesitation and once the Privy Council ruled in their favour, she never for a moment doubted that Emily Murphy would get the job she wanted and deserved. "I feel a bit of a humbug," she said at the time. "Mrs. Murphy is doing all the work (of the Persons Case) but I do support the cause."

In June of 1931, just after returning from a national WCTU conference in Toronto, Louise McKinney collapsed and died. It was thought that the strain of chairing most of the sessions had just been too much. She was only 63. There was an outpouring of praise from all sides but especially from her beloved WCTU. The national newsletter contained tribute after tribute, and at the funeral, some 100 WCTU members from all over Canada sat in a block in the church. As they filed past the grave later, each dropped a small white ribbon onto the casket, the white ribbon being the WCTU symbol of purity and faith.

chapter eighteen

Irene Parlby, Last But Not Least

Irene Parlby was known as The Honourable Mrs. Parlby in government circles; she was Mrs. Parlby to the women who looked to her for leadership; she was eventually Dr. Parlby when the University of Alberta gave her an honorary degree in 1935, but to her husband she was Irenee. That's Irene pronounced the old way, the way that means Queen in Greek. That's how Walter thought of her – as a Queen.

Theirs is such a lovely love story that it's hard to get onto the official part of her life, and it's probably why she was always torn between her public duty and her private life. For instance, when she was asked by Prime Minister R.B. Bennett to be one of three Canadian representatives to the League of Nations meeting in Geneva in the fall of 1930, she very nearly turned him down "because it was harvest time." She would be needed on the farm at this the busiest time of all. Besides, son Humphrey and his fiancée Beatrice Buckley were to be married soon. How could she possibly get away at this time?

Walter said she must go. He'd manage. Humphrey and Bea could wait a few months. They'd be OK. So she went. And when she wrote later telling Walter all about the speeches that were made, the well-known personalities that were there, the glittering ball which she had attended, Walter read the letter aloud to the young pair and then said, his voice choked with emotion, "Do you know what's the best part of all this?"

"The best part is that she's my wife."

"He was so proud of her," Bea said years later.

Even their first meeting was the stuff of which romantic novels are made. In 1896, Irene Marryat came to Canada from England to visit friends in what was then called the North West Territories. It

Not your average homesteader, Irene Parlby (left) had a privileged upbringing in England and India.

Photo Courtesy Glenbow Archives
NA-2204-11

was to be one big lark as far as she was concerned – a chance to see the country her great uncle Captain Frederick Marryat had written about in one of his books called *The Settlers of Canada*. And lark it was. "My first drive from Lacombe which was the nearest train station 30 miles away," she wrote later, "was a thing of vivid memories, tumbling out of one mudhole into another, doubling up teams to get through, dropping into a creek and praying the bridge of poles was somewhere under the water, and we might be lucky enough to hit the middle of it in the waning light of a summer evening, arriving at the ranch about 11:30 pm, tired out but thrilled with a feeling of adventure."

The friends were the Westheads. They lived a few miles away from two young British bachelors, Walter and Edward Parlby.

Irene and husband Walter who studied Greek at Oxford before emigrating to Canada.

Photo Courtesy Glenbow Archives NA-2925-3

One day when Alix Westhead and Irene went for a drive, they just happened to pass by the Parlby place where Walter Parlby just happened to be standing beside the lake in front of his place. And that was it. Irene and Walter were married the next spring. Irene didn't visit England again until son Humphrey was born two years later.

Such is the power of wide-open spaces and the lure of adventure.

They were not the kind of homesteaders that we usually read about, those who came to Canada to escape poverty or persecution in other lands. Walter Parlby had his Master's degree in Classics from Oxford and liked nothing better than to sit down with his Greek classics and read a bit every day. Irene had grown up in England and India with all the perks that go with privilege – governesses, finishing school in Switzerland, travel, but she didn't seem to miss that life. In fact, she said about her new home, "Everything was fresh and the world seemed so young and interesting. Seeing a country in the making is an interest not given to everyone."

As part of married life, Irene joined the Alix Country Women's Club and was soon elected secretary. "Little did I think as I accepted the position that I was taking the initial step that was going to plunge me into many years of public life, for which I had no ambition at all."

She may not have had the ambition for public life but she had the ability. She was an educated Englishwoman who had both the educational and social background to hold her own in political circles. What's more, she could see it was her duty. Someone had to speak up for rural women and their children.

In 1915, farmers organized under the banner of the United Farmers of Alberta. The women formed an auxiliary and the Alix Country Women's Club became Auxiliary #1. Not for long, however, did they remain an auxiliary. When Irene Parlby agreed to become provincial president of the "auxiliary", she discouraged the idea that they should be an adjunct to the men's organization. Women in rural areas had sufficient common cause to justify their own interest group, she argued, and was supported in that opinion by the UFA leader, Henry Wise Wood. "Be active and assertive," he urged. "Agricultural people have suffered more than other classes. You women have a task to perform."

He was always a great fan of Mrs. Parlby's. "When the British are at their best, you can't beat them, and Mrs. Parlby is English at its very best," he once said.

"The woman, in a battle of fists or guns, may not be as great a power as a man, but a woman behind a vote is every bit as useful as a man."
- Irene Parlby

Irene Parlby, Minister without Portfolio for the UFA government, sitting among the suits after the 1921 election.

Photo Courtesy Glenbow Archives NA-2204-4

The auxiliary soon became its own person – the United Farm Women of Alberta, the UFWA.

During the next five years, Mrs. Parlby had to leave her family and garden behind more and more as she travelled through the province encouraging members of the UFWA to advocate for rural hospitals, public health nurses, travelling health clinics for the more remote rural areas, rural libraries, more and better schools, more and better cooperation in all areas of life.

In 1921, the UFA decided to become a political party and run candidates in the upcoming election. Mrs. Parlby was asked to let her name stand in the riding of Lacombe and because no one, especially Mrs. Parlby, gave the UFA party much hope of success, she agreed. Some weeks later, the UFA surprised everyone and swept into office in one of those all-or-nothing elections that Alberta periodically dishes up. Irene Parlby was suddenly an MLA. "I didn't know whether to laugh or cry," she said later. Not only that but the premier, Herbert Greenfield, named her Minister Without Portfolio, making her the second woman in the British Empire to hold a cabinet position in a provincial government.

(The other one was Mary Ellen Smith from British Columbia who was named a cabinet minister just months before Parlby.)

From then on, any pictures taken of the Cabinet show a sea of men in dark suits with one female in their midst, a woman with calm eyes and a straight back, a woman who always wore a hat – black in the winter, white in the summer. That's what she decided early on. There wasn't time to coordinate and fuss about her clothes. She would stick with black and white, which she did, beautifully.

At first, it was all a bit sudden and a bit much, but Mrs. Parlby rose to the occasion, patiently working away at problems that affected the rural population. Much better than Nellie McClung or Emily Murphy who preferred to see things change *now*, Irene Parlby accepted the molasses-like slowness of government with its need to assess and reassess before doing anything. "Evolution cannot be brought about by the use of dynamite," she said.

Through it all, she gained a reputation for straight talk. A newspaper reporter once said, "She has none of the tricks of the trade. When she speaks to her constituents, she neglects to illustrate her points with funny stories. She makes her hearers neither laugh nor cry. She makes them think."

Imagine.

She won the Lacombe riding again in 1926, went back into the cabinet as Minister Without Portfolio and sat among the suits. When Emily called in 1927, she gladly added her signature to the petition. Of course, she would. It was her Duty. Besides, Emily wanted the job, and she'd paid her dues. Just because Irene would rather walk barefoot over coals than go one step further into politics didn't mean she wouldn't support other women.   Irene Parlby finished off her third term as Minister without Portfolio in the UFA government, but in 1935 she said a firm no and declined any suggestion that she should try for a fourth. Just as well, since the Alberta electorate did one of its famous turnarounds and elected William Aberhart's Social Credit party. Not a single UFA member survived the upset.

Not at all upset, Irene went back to her garden, watched her grandchildren grow up, took part in her community and lived to be 97 years old. About her political career, she once said she'd make a bonfire of all her official papers and correspondence and once the fire burnt high, she'd dance merrily about it. Perhaps that's exactly what she did because her files at archives and museums are much slimmer than the ones for the other Famous Five.

"If politics mean... the effort to secure through legislative action better conditions of life for the people, greater opportunities for our children and other people's children... then it most assuredly is a woman's job just as much as it is a man's job."
- Irene Parlby, 1928

chapter nineteen

In Conclusion, A Thank You from the Author

Dear Emily Murphy,

I want to thank you for bringing off the Persons Case. I've seen the files of letters you wrote and the copious notes you made about Canadian and British laws so I know this wasn't an easy task. Besides that, you took a lot of guff in the process. Thank you for sticking with it. It was important; you were right.

My mother should have been the one to thank you first. She was 18 years old in 1929, in training at a normal school to become a teacher. She should have cared about personhood because she certainly had to be a person once she faced a classroom full of students in every grade at every level. But she thought the whole personhood thing was a piffle. Just words, she said.

She said the same thing when I became interested in the women's liberation movement in the 1960s. It's just words, she said. Besides, who wants to be known as a women's libber? she said.

Isn't that just words? I said. So we agreed to stop using certain words around one another.

But I am older now. More than ever, I know that words matter. If women weren't "persons" in the eyes of one section of the BNA Act, then they weren't persons all the way down the line. If they weren't persons who could be senators, then how could they be expected to be aldermen or school principals or ministers of the church or bank managers or equal partners in business or marriage? They were women. Therefore, they were less somehow. Perception is everything. Attitude is everywhere.

You were never less, Emily. How did you manage to avoid all the conditioning that most other women got in your day? How come you didn't worry about being called "bossy" or a "battleaxe?" You were both of the above if I read the history books right, yet you went ahead anyway. Why didn't those labels stop you? Instead, you bullied that Persons Case through hell and high water and won the war of words. After 1929, women were persons in law as well as fact. Good for you.

Mind you, you lost the battle. No Senate appointment for you, even though you deserved and wanted it. Such is the small-mindedness of politics, but here's where the law of unexpected results kicks in. Turns out that your exclusion from the Senate so many years ago makes your story even more compelling now, makes your contribution even more amazing. You didn't benefit personally from your work on the Persons Case. What's more, you didn't whine, didn't murmur one word about discrimination toward certain persons. Just pursued your course as full-fledged person to the end. Amazing. Thank you.

Yours Very Sincerely, Nancy Millar

the persons case, a quick summary

WHY?

Emily Murphy was named a police magistrate for a Women's Court in Edmonton in 1916. On her first day on the job, a lawyer challenged her right to be there because she was not a "person" according to the BNA Act (the British North America Act.) That argument was cleared up a year later when the Alberta government ruled that women were persons as far as provincial law was concerned.

However, the definition of persons came back to haunt Emily when women's groups across Canada forwarded her name to government officials as someone who should be appointed to the Senate. No matter how many people supported her appointment and no matter how many times her name was forwarded, the answer always came back that women were not persons as defined by the act concerning the appointment of senators. Therefore, they could not be appointed to the Senate. Three different prime ministers and administrations took that stand. "The same old rigmarole," Emily said.

WHAT?

Section 24 of the BNA Act said, "The Governor General shall from time to time summon qualified persons to the Senate." Never had the word "persons" in that section been interpreted to mean female persons.

WHO?

Emily Murphy learned of a clause in the Supreme Court of Canada Act that allowed five persons acting as a unit to petition the Supreme Court for an interpretation of any part of the BNA Act. In 1927, she assembled Nellie McClung, Irene Parlby, Louise McKinney and Henrietta Muir Edwards to join her in a petition that eventually asked, "Does the word 'persons' in Section 24 of the BNA Act include female persons?"

WHEN?

The following year, the Supreme Court of Canada ruled No. The BNA Act, written in 1867, was based on British common law, they argued. Under British common law, women were persons in matters of pain and penalty but not in matters of rights and privileges. Therefore, the Fathers of Confederation would not have intended that women be admitted to the Senate. That was the chief argument. They did not attempt to explain why the Parliament of Canada had been able to pass laws allowing women to vote and run for office in federal elections. By 1928, women had had both those rights for some years. It was only the Senate that remained a male-only institution. Where was the justice in that, Emily asked, or the good sense? If the Senate was a necessary part of Canadian government, then it should be representative of all Canadians. All persons, as it were.

THEN? When the Supreme Court of Canada said no, Emily assembled her gang once again and they sent an appeal off to the Privy Council of England, then the highest court of appeal for Canada.

SO? October 18, 1929, five judges of the Privy Council of England ruled that Yes, Canadian women were persons, so there. Essentially, they said that things change, that the BNA Act was not set in stone but could change with the times. And yes, women could be senators.

HOW SOON? Not soon enough for Emily Murphy. Cairine Wilson of Ontario was the first woman named to the Senate. Emily admitted to being "ruffled in spirit." Everyone expected her to be first but there's more than one way to keep a good woman down. She never did get the call and died four years later.

WHY NOT? There are those who say she would have caused too much ruckus, laughed too loud, challenged too much. After all, one of her favourite saying was "Whenever I don't know whether to fight or not, I fight."

WHY THEN? Alberta didn't a get a woman senator until 50 years later when Joe Clark named Martha Bielish of Warspite to the Senate.

WHAT NOW? "I was not a person for the first three years of my life. It was only in 1929 because of the enormous efforts of such women as Nellie McClung and Emily Murphy that Canadian women were finally legally recognizcd as 'persons'. Of course, at three, I wasn't aware that I had suddenly been promoted into person-hood. Certainly my mother and aunts never saw themselves as inferior, or non-persons, whatever the asinine law might have said."

Margaret Laurence from *Dance on the Earth*, 1989

timelines for the famous five

Emily Murphy

1868	March 14, born in Cookstown, Ontario, to Isaac and Emily Ferguson.
1887	married Rev. Arthur Murphy. Four daughters born to the marriage – two died in childhood, two survived – Kathleen and Evelyn.
1898	family moved to England where Arthur served as missionary. Emily began her writing career under the pseudonym of Janey Canuck.
1901	family returned to Canada. Emily had her first book published, *The Impressions of Janey Canuck Abroad*.
1903	moved to Swan River, Manitoba, where Arthur changed jobs. Became a timber and mining entrepreneur. Emily wrote for magazines.
1907	moved to Edmonton. Arthur continued mining and timber business, Emily quickly became active in social causes for women.
1910	Emily became the first woman member of a hospital board in Edmonton and then turned up on local boards and committees for the next 20 years.
1910, 1912, 1914	three more books from the pen of Janey Canuck: *Janey Canuck in the West, Open Trails and Seeds of Pine*, all of them sketches of life in western Canada.
1911	the first version of a dower act to protect women's rights in matrimonial property was passed by the Alberta legislature, thanks in large part to Emily Murphy and Henrietta Muir Edwards.
1913	became president of the Canadian Women's Press Club. Through the years, served on the executive of at least 20 other women's professional and volunteer organizations, among them the National Council of

Women and the Federated Women's Institutes.

1916   appointed a police magistrate in a special Women's Court in Edmonton, the first woman to hold such a position in the British Empire. On her first day in court, she was told she was not a person according to Section 24 of the BNA Act and therefore couldn't be a judge.

1919   women's organizations across Canada began submitting Emily Murphy's name as a candidate for the Senate. Once again, she was told she was not a person.

1922   under her own name wrote *The Black Candle*, a book about the alarming drug trade in Canada.

1920s   one of Emily Murphy's brothers found an obscure clause in the Supreme Court of Canada Act that would allow five "persons" acting as a unit to ask for an interpretation of any part of the BNA Act. Emily seized upon the chance and picked her co-appellants: Nellie McClung, Louise McKinney, Henrietta Muir Edwards and Irene Parlby.

1927   the five women met in Edmonton and signed a petition to be sent to the Supreme Court asking for an interpretation of the word persons in Section 24. Did it mean female persons as well as male persons?

1928   the Supreme Court of Canada considered the question and said no, it does not. The original intent of the law as enacted in 1867 did not include women in the meaning of persons in Section 24, they declared.

1928   the five women met again and agreed to appeal the decision of the Supreme Court. They sent it to the final court of appeal which was then the Privy Council of England.

1929   October 18, five judges of the Privy Council in London reversed the Canadian decision and said, yes, Canadian women were persons and therefore eligible to be called to the Senate.

1929   women of Canada waited for Emily Murphy to be named the first woman senator.

1930   she wasn't named the first senator. Cairine Wilson, a longtime Liberal supporter from Ontario, was chosen.

1931   Emily resigned from her position as magistrate for the city of Edmonton in order to catch up with her writing and speaking assignments.

1933   October 27, she died suddenly in her sleep, the result of a heart attack complicated by diabetes. She was 65. Survived by husband Arthur who died in 1962; daughter Evelyn who never married, and daughter Kathleen, her husband Cleave Kenwood, and their daughter Emily Doris.

Nellie McClung

1873   born October 20, in Chatsworth, Ontario, sixth child of the Mooney family.

1880   family moved to the Souris valley, Manitoba

1896   August 25, married Wes McClung and moved to Manitou, Manitoba

1908   wrote *Sowing Seeds in Danny*, her first and most popular novel

1911   family moved to Winnipeg. Four children by then, Jack, Florence, Paul and Horace, The fifth, Mark, was born later that year.

1911-1914   became ever more involved in social causes, especially prohibition and votes for women through the WCTU, working conditions in factories, legal rights of women.

1914   played the part of the premier in a famous Mock Parliament on why men should not be allowed to vote. Brought down the house and eventually the government.

1914   Wes was transferred to Edmonton with his insurance business and Nellie transferred her feminist causes. Same causes, different location.

1914   Nellie wrote her only nonfiction book, *In Times Like These*, a very angry book about women's place in the scheme of things.

1915   son Jack went to war. Nellie grieved his absence and his loss of innocence.

1915   Alberta men voted to prohibit the sale of liquor.
        Women didn't yet have the right to vote.

1916   women in Manitoba got the vote, then Saskatchewan,
        then Alberta. Nellie had a finger in all pies.

1917   toured the United States, sometimes appearing for
        church groups, in chatauquas, in theatres. The toast of
        towns in Canada and the U.S.

1918   attended the Canadian Methodist Assembly and tried
        to persuade the church to allow female ordained
        ministers. The church resisted.

1918   son Jack returned safely from the war, never spoke of
        it. Nellie added peace to her busy agenda.

1920   most women got the right to vote in federal elections.

1921   elected as a Liberal MLA for Edmonton. Sat as loyal
        opposition to the UFA party but voted pretty well as
        her feminist inclinations dictated.

1923   the family moved to Calgary. Nellie commuted back
        and forth to Edmonton.

1923   prohibition was repealed, and liquor was available by
        1924. Nellie couldn't believe that women would use
        their hard won vote in such a negative way.

1926   Nellie sought reelection as an MLA in Calgary, was
        defeated by a slim 60 votes, likely because of her
        staunch opposition to the liquor trade.

1926   went back to her writing. In her lifetime, she wrote 16
        books, innumerable articles and speeches.

1927   gladly joined Emily Murphy in the Persons Case.

1929   celebrated her newly ordained personhood. Said
        she'd always suspected she was a person.

1933   Wes retired from the insurance business and they
        moved to Victoria, BC.

1935   finished the first part of her autobiography, *Clearing
        in the West*.

1936   United Church finally agreed to the ordination of
        women.

1936   she became the first woman appointed to the Board of Governors for the CBC.

1938   went to Geneva as Canadian representative to the League of Nations meeting.

1938   was the only member of the Famous Five to attend the unveiling of a plaque in the hall next to the Senate chamber honouring the Persons Case. Irene Parlby was still living but not able to attend.

1945   finished the story of her life with *The Stream Runs Fast*, the second part of her autobiography.

1946   she and Wes celebrated their 50th wedding anniversary.

1951   Sept. 1, died at age 78. Buried in Victoria, B.C. Survived by her husband Wes; daughter Florence Atkinson and her husband and children; sons Paul, Mark and Horace, their wives and children. Son Jack predeceased her. His wife and children survived her as well.

Irene Parlby

1868   January 9, born in England to privileged Marryat family, grew up there and in India.

1886   at age 18, "came out" at debutante ball with other young women of aristocracy.

1897   visited western Canada as guest of Alix and Charles Westhead who lived near Lacombe in the Northwest Territories.

1898   married Walter Coventry Hall Parlby, a neighbor of the Westheads. Settled down to become a pioneer rancher's wife.

1899   only child Humphrey born.

1905   Alberta became a province and the area east of Lacombe became known as Alix, named for the Parlby's friend. The Marryats from England decided to follow their daughter to the Alix area as well. There, they built a big house that became the community social centre.

1909   the United Farmers of Alberta organization was

formed to look after the concerns of farmers. Walter Parlby was 1st president of the Alix chapter.

1913   Irene agreed to serve as secretary of the Country Women's Club of Alix, a club formed to provide social and educational occasions for farm women.

1915   a UFA women's auxiliary was formed. Irene didn't like the idea of being an "auxiliary" but she saw it as her duty to join and add her voice to the need for rural reform.

1916   the women's auxiliary became independent of the men's organization and set itself up as the United Farm Women's Association. Irene became 1st provincial president.

1920   she was named as a member of the University of Alberta Board of Governors.

1921   she agreed to let her name stand as a candidate for the newly organized UFA political party. She never expected that either the UFA or she would be elected. They both were.

1921   the new premier Herbert Greenfield named her Minister Without Portfolio in his new cabinet, making her the second woman in the British Empire to serve as a cabinet minister and the first in Alberta. Nellie McClung sat with the Opposition across the floor but they often worked together on laws that related to women and children.

1924   she toured Europe, especially the Scandinavian countries, to study their methods of education and cooperative agricultural projects.

1925   sponsored the Minimum Wage for Women Act and continued to work on behalf of women, children and rural Albertans.

1926 & 1930   reelected as MLA for the Lacombe constituency. Continued as Minister Without Portfolio in the Cabinet. Missed her ally in the Opposition – Nellie McClung.

1927   signed Emily Murphy's Persons petition to the Supreme Court of Canada.

1930 represented Canada as one of three official delegates at the League of Nations meeting in Geneva, Switzerland

1935 happily retired from politics and went home to tend her garden, her family and her community.

1935 received an Honorary Doctor of Laws from the Univeristy of Alberta.

1965 July 12, died in Alix at the age of 97.
Survived by son Humphrey, daughter-in-law Bea and three grandchildren, Geoffrey, Gerald and Susan.

Henrietta Muir Edwards

1849 December 18, born to wealthy Muir family in Montreal

1874 as an extension of her religious belief in "good works," she established a residence and reading room for young working women in Montreal. A YWCA forerunner.

1875 put out a newsletter of advice for working women, Women's Work in Canada. Financed some of her social work through china painting.

1876 married Dr. Oliver Cromwell Edwards.

1883 moved with husband and two children, Alice and Muir, to Indian Head in what is now Saskatchewan where Oliver served as doctor for Indian reservations in the area. Another daughter, Margaret, born two years later.

1890 Oliver suffered health problems so the family moved back to Montreal and then to Ottawa.

1893 Henrietta worked with Lady Aberdeen, wife of the Governor General, to organize the National Council of Women in Canada. Became 1st Convener of the Standing Committee on Laws, a position she held until her death.

1893 painted a set of china for the Canadian Art Exhibit at the World's Fair in Chicago.

1897 aided and abetted Lady Aberdeen in forming the Victorian Order of Nurses to serve health needs in frontier areas.

1897   served as president of the Ottawa YWCA through the building of new headquarters.

1903   family moved back to the west, this time to the Blood Indian Reserve near Fort Macleod, Alberta

1909   served as delegate to the once-every-five-years national conference of the National Council of Women in Toronto. NCW went with her wherever she lived.

1910   a dower act was passed in the AB legislature. It didn't go nearly as far as either Henrietta Muir Edwards or Emily Murphy would have liked but it was a first step in protecting the rights of married women.

1913   daughter Margaret died in childbirth.

1915   Oliver died and Henrietta moved to nearby Fort Macleod where she lived with her sister Amelia.

1917   Henrietta's handbook on the Legal Status of Women in Canada was published by the Canadian government. A similar publication relating to Alberta laws was published the same year and revised in 1921.

1918   son Muir, one of the first four professors at the new University of Alberta, died during the flu epidemic. He had volunteered to care for sick students and was struck down himself.

1927   Henrietta joined the other four women to challenge th BNA Act. The case became known as Edwards vs the Attorney General because the names of the Famous Five were listed in alphabetical order and Henrietta happened to be on top of the list.

1931   November 10, died at the age of 82 years. Buried with Oliver, Margaret and Muir in Edmonton.
Survived by daughter Alice and her husband Claude W. E. Gardiner and their two children, Oliver Ernest (Gard) and Claudia; daughter-in-law Edna Evelyn and children Douglas, Muriel and Joyce; her son-in-law Alexander George Stewart and their child, Alexander Graeme Stewart.

Louise McKinney

1868   October 22, born at Frankville, Ontario, seventh child of ten in the Crummy family.

1885   wanted to be a doctor but settled for teaching. Attended normal school in Ottawa.

1886-1892   taught school in the Frankville area.

1893   moved to North Dakota to teach there.

1894   increased her involvement with the WCTU, began to travel with WCTU organizers to establish new chapters of the organization.

1896   married James McKinney, a kindred soul in the Christian determination to rid the world of alcohol.

1897   son Willard born, named for Frances Willard, the founder of the WCTU in the US.

1903   moved to Claresholm, Alberta. James McKinney immediately set to work to build a church, Louise began organizing chapters of the WCTU.

1904   through constant travelling and letter writing, Louise had 20 WCTU chapters up and going.

1907   she became a vice president of the national WCTU and attended the World WCTU conference in Boston.

1912   Alberta and Saskatchewan were divided into two separate districts of the WCTU. Louise continued as president of the Alberta district.

1913   she attended the World WCTU convention in Brooklyn, New York

1915   the male voters of Alberta voted to outlaw liquor. Prohibition was a fact. The WCTU couldn't have been more delighted. By 1916, the appropriate legislation was in place to totally prohibit the sale of liquor.

1916   the women of Alberta got the right to vote, thanks in large part to the WCTU and Louise McKinney who worked steadfastly through the years to get the vote for women.

1917   Louise ran as a non-partisan candidate in the provincial election and was elected. Two women were elected that year but the other one, Roberta

MacAdams, was not able to be present on the opening day of the Legislature so Louise got the distinction of "first woman" to sit in a provincial legislature in the British Empire. Roberta MacAdams joined her as soon as she got home from her duties as a nursing sister overseas.

1920　Louise attended the World WCTU convention in London, England.

1921　she was defeated in her second bid for election, mostly because of her rigid non-drinking and non-smoking platform.

1923　prohibition was defeated in a provincial referendum. Women, it turned out, didn't always vote the way the WCTU thought they should. By the following year, bars were open again and the WCTU never recovered.

1925　Louise was the only western woman to sign the Basis of Union when three churches joined to form the United Church of Canada.

1927　Louise signed Emily Murphy's petition for personhood.

1928　attended the World WCTU convention in Lausanne, Switzerland.

1931　as acting president of the Canadian WCTU, she chaired many of the sessions at the national meeting in Toronto. Named 1st vice president of the World WCTU.

1931　July 10, died two weeks after the Toronto meeting, aged 63. Survived by her husband James McKinney, son Willard, his wife Mable and their two children, G. Norman and Lorna.

aunt hetty remembered

Kim Smith, a grandniece of Henrietta Muir Edwards remembered "Aunt Hetty" at a luncheon sponsored by the Famous Five Foundation on January 17, 1997, in Calgary, Alberta. The Famous Five Foundation exists to honour the Famous Five and carry on their work.

Aunt Hetty was a practical strong woman both. No-nonsense and down to business in both her professional and family life.

At a gathering of family members, a squabble arose among the young cousins present at the gathering. Several of the adults, including Aunt Hetty, intervened and admonished the children for their unseemly behavior. Upon being chastised, one of the youngest cousins was heard to cry, "But it's not fair!!!!!!"

A definite hush came over the rest of the children and the adults as well. After all, this was a period in time when children were expected to be "seen and not heard."

Aunt Hetty calmly walked over to the young girl (whose eyes grew wider with each step that brought Aunt Hetty closer to her) and took her by the hand. She sat the child down and proceeded to have the child explain to her, calmly and rationally, why she felt the situation was not fair. After listening seriously to the child, Aunt Hetty reminded her that whining and complaining had never been known to solve any injustice in the world and if she truly, truly, believed that "it's not fair," then the solution rested solely with her. She had best put her mind to figuring out a way that would make the situation fair.

In that instant, a young girl, whether she realized it or not, was given the gift of empowerment. She was shown that she could take control, solve a problem and make a difference.

I am incredibly proud to have Henrietta Muir Edwards as a branch of my family and I would like to take this opportunity to thank the Famous Five Foundation for their work in reminding all Canadians how important the efforts of these dedicated women were and how, without their strength and determination, we might still be sitting back crying, "It's not fair."

acknowledgements

I want, most of all, to acknowledge the Famous Five who took so much guff in their lifetimes to accomplish what we take entirely for granted. Thank you.

Then I want to acknowledge the women who made this book possible. They too admire their foremothers – be they their own mothers and grandmothers or the Famous Five specifically. And they too want their daughters and granddaughters, their sons and grandsons, to know and honour the work of women in building Canada. It was, and is, a shared task.

Thus my heartfelt thanks go to the following who willingly supported me and the Western Heritage Centre in the publication of this book:

- Gwen Thorssen, first of all, who when I put the project before her, said, "Of course, Nancy. Just let me make a few phone calls." As a result of her phone calls, Doris Govier, Carol Diamond, Jean Minchin, Donna McGown, Peggy Rose Fowler-Ferguson, Jean Mekitiak and Yolande Jones added their support to the project.
- Lois Alger also said "Of course" when I told her about the book.
- Mary Guichon said, "Certainly, but you'll have to come to lunch with me to explain it fully." Thus did I get support for the project and a lunch. What more could I ask?
- Margaret Randall McCready, Norma Farquharson and Beverley Bennett were equally willing. I am humbled by such support.

Also, it must be mentioned that Donna Livingstone, Director of the Western Heritage Centre, also said "Yes" immediately. Women's history is not always equally represented among talk of ranches and cowboys and bushels per acre. (Sorry, hectares.) Thus a book on women's history offered some balance.

In fact, I'm so pleased that this story is finally being printed, that it will finally be available for schools, women's groups and individuals who just want to know the story, that I'm ready to thank one and all. Why not? Thank you all!

Nancy Millar

bibliography

1. Sanders, Bryne Hope. *Emily Murphy Crusader*. Toronto: The Macmillan Co. of Canada, 1945

2. Norris, Marjorie. *A Leaven of Ladies*. Calgary, Alberta: Detselig Publishing, 1995

3. Warne, Randi. *Literature as Pulpit*. Waterloo, Ontario: Wilfred University Press, 1993

4. Prentice, Alison et al. *Canadian Women, A History*. Toronto: Harcourt Brace Javanovich

5. Savage, Candace. *Our Nell*. Saskatoon, SK: Western Producer Prairie Books, 1979

6. Cormack, Barabara Villy. *Perennieals and Politics*

7. Silverman, Elaine Leslau. *The Last Best West*. Calgary: Fifth House Publishing, 1998

8. Dempsey, Hugh, ed. *The Best From Alberta History*. Saskatoon: Western Producer Prairie Books, 1981

9. Rasmussen, Rasmussen, Savage and Wheeler. *A Harvest Yet to Reap*. Toronto: The Women's Press, 1976

10. Hallet, Mary E. *Firing the Heather*. Saskatoon: Fifth House Publishers, 1993

11. Rex, Kay. *No Daughter of Mine*. Toronto: Cedar Cave Publishing, 1995

12. James, Donna. *Emily Murphy, the Canadians series*. Don Mills, ON: Fitzhenry and Whiteside, 1977

13. Benham, Mary Lile. *Nellie McClung, the Canadians series*. Don Mills, On: Fitzhenry and Whiteside, 1975

14. Francis and Smith, eds. *Readings in Canadian History, Post Confederation*. Holt, Rinehart and Winston of Canada Ltd, 1990

15. Cleverdon, Catherine. *The Women Suffrage Movement in Canada*. Toronto: University of Toronto Press, 1978

books by nellie mcclung

1. Sowing Seeds in Danny, 1908

2. The Second Chance, 1910

3. The Black Creek Stopping House, 1912

4. In Times Like These, 1915. Reprint 1975

5. The Next of Kin, 1917

6. Three Times and Out, 1918

7. Purple Springs, 1921

8. When Christmas Crossed the Peace, 1923

9. Painted Fires, 1925

10. All We Like Sheep, 1930

11. Be Good To Yourself, 1930

12. Flowers for the Living, 1931

13. Clearing in the West: My Own Story, 1935

14. Leaves From Lantern Lane, 1936

15. More Leaves From Lantern Lane, 1937

16. The Stream Runs Fast: My Own Story, 1945

books by emily murphy

1. The Impressions of Janey Canuck Abroad, 1901

2. Janey Canuck in the West, 1910

3. Open Trails, 1912

4. Seeds of Pine, 1914

5. The Black Candle, 1922

6. Bishop Bompas, 1929

index

About the Author

Nancy Millar has been a fan of the Famous Five for about 100 years, she says. She's also keen on the history of Alberta and Canada generally and to that end has written two other books in the history field. The first, *Remember Me As You Pass By*, uses Alberta graveyards as the entry to Alberta's past. The second, *Once Upon a Tomb*, uses Canadian graveyards as the passport to our national past.

"I've been called a good story teller," she says, "which is a good thing since history is a story."

Nancy Millar has lived in Alberta all her life but still has hopes for the south of France.